Alternative Futures for Global Food and Agriculture

Please cite this publication as:
OECD (2016), *Alternative Futures for Global Food and Agriculture*, OECD Publishing, Paris.
http://dx.doi.org/10.1787/9789264247826-en

ISBN 978-92-64-24775-8 (print)
ISBN 978-92-64-24782-6 (PDF)

Photo credits: Cover © weerapat1003 - Fotolia.com

Corrigenda to OECD publications may be found on line at: *www.oecd.org/about/publishing/corrigenda.htm*.

Foreword

Will our global food system be able to feed nine billion people without destroying sensitive ecosystems or social coherence? Can agricultural productivity keep apace with rapidly increasing demand while faced with significant and unpredictable challenges such as climate change, livestock diseases and other factors which escalate production costs? Will farming be a profitable business in the coming decades, helping rural areas to develop and maintain their role within economies and livelihoods? Such fundamental questions are pivotal to any discussion of the future of agricultural markets and the food system. However, the numerous uncertain and changing factors which surround these concerns can pose immense challenges for the development of effective policy and industry strategies to address them.

Scenario analysis provides an alternative approach to address an inherently uncertain future which model projections alone cannot completely assess. While they do not represent "forecasts" or "projections", and are subject to numerous caveats and uncertainties, scenarios provide a tool to consider different possible futures that take political, economic, technological and other "known unknowns" into account. As such, scenario analysis forms a valuable basis for the consideration of more adaptive strategies. The aim of this report is to explore three examples of potential "futures" which may await food and agricultural systems. These alternative pictures of global development aim at enabling the constructive discussion, design and implementation of public and private strategies which are sufficiently robust to achieve desired outcomes, regardless of how the future unfolds.

Three alternative scenarios were jointly developed by OECD and non-member ministry participants at two OECD Workshops on Long-Term Scenarios for Food and Agriculture that took place in December 2013 and September 2014. These discussions were complemented by additional literature, by quantitative results derived from a set of global economic models, and information obtained from workshop participants via a dedicated electronic discussion forum. The scenarios represent alternative pathways that agricultural markets may follow in the lead up to 2050. They differ along four key dimensions including the degree of co-operation between regions and countries, societal attitudes towards sustainability, the focus of technological developments and the overall system stability. These scenarios are not designed to represent the "most likely" outlook, but rather to contain relevant aspects of possible developments in order to enable constructive consideration of challenges and policy opportunities.

The scenarios developed within this report merit future use, refinement and questioning, both within the OECD and elsewhere. Where possible, they should be "regionalised" or even "nationalised" by countries, with the involvement of relevant stakeholders, to allow for the provision of more tailored policy advice. Further discussions on the potential pathways and their implications for the food and agriculture system, as well as for public and private strategies, will also need to involve non-governmental stakeholders.

Chapter 1 of this report outlines the three key trends that frame the challenges facing food and agriculture, before presenting the three long-term scenarios for the world in 2050 and exploring the development of agricultural markets within these alternative "futures". Chapter 2 considers seven challenges in depth within the context of these three scenarios. The performance of each in relation to the challenges to food and agriculture is then compared in order to facilitate the identification and discussion of strategies to manage risks and avail of future opportunities (Chapter 3).

This work has benefitted from financial support under the OECD-wide project on New Approaches to Economic Challenges, of which it forms an integral part. The report is based on a document (TAD/TC/CA/WP(2015)1/FINAL) declassified by the OECD Joint Working Party on Agriculture and Trade.

Acknowledgements

Martin von Lampe, of the OECD Directorate for Trade and Agriculture, is the lead author of this report and Frank van Tongeren provided general supervision to the project. Administrative and editorial assistance were provided by Martina Abderrahmane, Marina Giacalone-Belkadi, Michèle Patterson and Clara Thompson-Lipponen.

The participants to the two workshops as well as delegates to the OECD Joint Working Party on Agriculture and Trade provided invaluable input, and indeed have collectively designed and analysed the scenarios of this report.

Many other individuals contributed in some form to this work. While some provided or reviewed text, data or analysis, others acted as facilitators or provided valuable expertise to the two workshops mentioned above. Acknowledging individual colleagues for their contributions always risks missing others, but particular gratitude for their active contributions to this work is extended to: Marcel Adenäuer, OECD; Jesús Antón, OECD; Jonathan Brooks, OECD; David Coates, Convention on Biological Diversity; David Cooper, Convention on Biological Diversity; Ian Crute, UK Foresight; Anna Davies, Trinity College Dublin; Koen Deconinck, OECD; Rob Dellink, OECD; Ruth Delzeit, OECD; Hubertus Gay, OECD; Delia Grace, International Livestock Research Institute; Jared Greenville, OECD; Peter Griffin, Axis Capital; Petr Havlik, International Institute of Applied Systems Analysis; Ada Ignaciuk, OECD; Hans Joehr, Nestec S.A.; Shingo Kimura, OECD; Roger Martini, OECD; Daniel Mason Dæ'Croz, International Food Policy Research Institute; Martin Mayer, PMP Conseil; Olga Melyukhina, OECD; Catherine Moreddu, OECD; Ignacio Perez-Dominguez, formerly OECD; Sherman Robinson, International Food Policy Research Institute; Mark Rosegrant, International Food Policy Research Institute; Pierre-Alain Schieb, Graduate School of Business; Erwin Schmid, University of Natural Resources and Life Sciences, Vienna; Elke Stehfest, Netherlands Environmental Assessment Agency; Andrzej Tabeau, LEI Wageningen UR; Hubo Valin, International Institute of Applied Systems Analysis; Dominique van der Mensbrugghe, formerly UN Food and Agriculture Organization; Bernd van der Meulen, Wageningen UR; Hans van Meijl, LEI Wageningen UR; Ken Webster, Ellen MacArthur Foundation; and Keith Wiebe, International Food Policy Research Institute.

Table of contents

Figures

Boxes

Executive summary

The global food system faces numerous challenges which will shape developments towards 2050. Feeding – and indeed nourishing – a growing, more affluent and increasingly demanding population while preserving sensitive ecosystems; increasing agricultural productivity growth while both adapting to and mitigating climate change and other threats; competing for access to increasingly limited land, water and other natural resources; and contributing to rural area well-being, to name just a few. Nevertheless, the future is not necessarily bleak, as beyond this daunting list of challenges lie crucial opportunities which should not be overlooked.

This study aims to provide essential insights into the possible futures, challenges and opportunities facing the food and agriculture systems, and to challenge assumptions regarding the development of, and linkages between, the different drivers and outcomes towards the middle of this century. To this end, three alternative scenarios are presented, each of which depicts alternative pathways which the world may follow in the period leading up to 2050:

- **"Individual, Fossil Fuel-Driven Growth"** portrays a world driven by sovereignty and self-sufficiency, characterised by the strong focus of individual countries and regions on economic growth and relatively less emphasis by governments or their citizens on environmental or social questions. Co-operation is limited to regional alliances and is driven by national interests rather than long-term geo-political visions. Technological developments are based on fossil fuel extraction.
- The **"Citizen-Driven, Sustainable Growth"** world, in which consumers and citizens drive individual countries to emphasise environmental and social protection. Global co-operation is relatively limited. Technologies are focused on natural resource savings and the preservation of the environment.
- The **"Fast, Globally-Driven Growth"** scenario illustrates a future which is characterised by a strong focus on international co-operation to achieve economic growth. Environmental issues receive less attention from governments or their citizens. Technologies flourish in many domains, particularly in the areas of food, feed and energy production, and are easily shared internationally.

The scenarios do not aim to portray the "most likely" outlook, but rather to enable the constructive discussion and identification of robust policy and private sector responses to the challenges which lie ahead. The report also addresses a number of questions, such as: What do the scenario outcomes imply for policy approaches which could help to ensure that future food and agricultural needs are met in an economically, environmentally and socially sustainable manner? How can joint action, be it public, private or public-private, improve outcomes? And how can international organisations such as the OECD best support and advance beneficial joint action?

Key findings

Food prices could well continue to rise

The scenarios discussed within this report suggest that the era of falling real agricultural prices, a key feature of the second half of the 20th century, may be over. Nevertheless, while some studies on the future of agriculture indicate that global markets may be under continued and significant stress, with significantly rising food prices, the outcomes of the OECD scenarios suggest that future price increases in these three cases should in fact remain more limited as productivity and yields continue to rise. This result is, however, due to the specifics of the three scenarios and of their quantification, and is therefore not a projection that would contradict other findings.

Farm incomes should also increase; however, agricultural sector contribution to GDP and employment will fall

For farmers around the world, an end to falling agricultural prices would create substantial opportunities and – in a context of further productivity growth – raise farm incomes. This is particularly the case in land-abundant regions, but also in Asia, where productivity and farm incomes lag behind other regions. Nevertheless, despite the positive prospect of increased earnings, the agricultural share of both GDP and employment are expected to shrink even further relative to the overall global economy, with labour mostly moving into expanding service and non-food manufacturing sectors. Moreover, while global food security may well improve in line with rising incomes, the degree and speed of progress varies dramatically between scenarios.

Trans-boundary livestock diseases and food safety risks will continue to remain a threat to global agriculture

This is particularly the case within the meat-rich Individual, Fossil Fuel-Driven Growth and Fast, Globally-Driven Growth scenarios. Risks related to food safety and trans-boundary diseases may be weaker in a Citizen-Driven, Sustainable Growth world given the reduced livestock production and other factors. Without international co-operation on food regulation and controls, however, these risks remain important.

Each scenario features its own priority challenges

Growth based largely on independent decision-making by countries and a high reliance on fossil energy, as is the case within the Individual, Fossil Fuel-Driven Growth scenario, could exacerbate food insecurity and food safety risks and increase pressure on the natural environment. Meanwhile, a world driven by sustainability-focused citizens, depicted by the Citizen-Driven, Sustainable Growth scenario, would feature major improvements in environmental performance but would challenge farmers to adopt more sustainable production methods and respond to changes in consumer behaviour. Finally, the Fast, Globally-Driven Growth scenario, which relies upon international co-operation, market efficiency and innovation to overcome natural resource constraints, could improve economic growth prospects for the majority of regions worldwide, yet could equally amplify risks related to climate change and threats to biodiversity. The majority of these challenges will develop differently across regions and time.

Nevertheless, all three "futures" see the environment being placed under increasing strain – albeit to varying extents

With the further expansion of agricultural land use and the growing use of farm inputs, notably in developing and emerging economies, the Individual, Fossil Fuel-Driven Growth and Fast, Globally-Driven Growth scenarios indicate serious threats to sensitive habitats and ecosystems, with potentially significant losses in biodiversity. Even in the Citizen-Driven, Sustainable Growth scenario, which features substantially reduced demand for meat and other livestock products, forests in Sub-Saharan Africa and Latin America would continue to decline without dedicated protective action – albeit at lower rates than in the two other scenarios. Agricultural greenhouse gas emissions and other pollutants could also continue to increase within all scenarios, even if more slowly than agricultural output and comparatively less in a Citizen-Driven, Sustainable Growth world.

Key recommendations

Versatile, comprehensive and robust strategies are required, not only involving governments but also private actors

The scenarios presented each suggest very different outcomes for some fundamental concerns. Policies need to be sufficiently robust, comprehensive and versatile to respond to an array of challenges across a diverse range of scenarios and thus ensure that future needs are consistently met in an economically, environmentally and socially sustainable manner. Public authorities' actions will also increasingly need to be complemented by private involvement. Five strategies are identified within the study for governments and private actors, where relevant:

- The **accelerated movement towards more sustainable lifestyles and consumption patterns**. This broadly involves all stakeholders in lifestyle changes, and can be achieved both by public policies, such as the reform of subsidy and tax systems and consumer awareness campaigns; and private sector initiatives, including voluntary standards and certification. The importance of region- and country-specific lifestyles and mindsets in this process should not be overlooked. Lifestyles differ across countries and can change over time, partly in response to public and private activities to provide food-related information.
- The **improved coherence of food market regulations across countries** is an essential component of a well-functioning international trade system which would in turn not only have the potential to raise incomes and productivity but to also cushion local and regional supply-side shocks and mitigate their adverse impacts on food security. Greater coherence may also enable costs reductions for producers and consumers, improved crisis management options and increased knowledge spill-overs. While international guidelines for regulations can facilitate coherence, there is a need for better identification of best practices for standard-setting and good regulatory practices.
- **Sustainable productivity growth**. Governments need to re-evaluate policies which pose obstacles to sustainable productivity growth. These include support for the use of fossil energy or other energy-intensive inputs in agricultural production and other sectors. Sustainable productivity growth also requires a well-functioning agricultural innovation system, involving both public and private actors. Finally, the concept of productivity growth needs to take the use of natural resources into account, including "common pool" resources such as fresh water and the emission of greenhouse gases. The development of related indicators is of key importance in this respect.
- **Improvements in infrastructure**, the improvement of its climate resilience included, result in less costly domestic transportation and information flows between agricultural actors, food processors, and consumers, in addition to better connections to international markets. As a

consequence, the efficiency of local and national markets is improved, supporting local and rural economies and enabling higher revenues for farmers yet lower prices for final consumers.

- **The improvement and broadening of agricultural risk management systems**, including insurance and banking systems and adapted and reliable tax and social security systems, will become increasingly critical for the management of volatile markets resulting from a multitude of weather, policy or technological shocks. Farm households, farm associations, insurers, other financial industries and governments all have key roles to play in this respect.

Opportunities for improving outcomes are not limited to changes in agricultural policies

Due to the multi-disciplinary nature of the challenges at hand, a wide range of policy areas will need to contribute to more robust strategies, including within up- and downstream industries as well as the general economy, education, health, environment and others. An increased focus on policy coherence across these policy fields is therefore indispensable.

There is significant scope for the enhancement of international co-operation in key areas

An increasing number of challenges will require international co-operation in future. These include global commons such as the climate and sustainability, international trade, regulatory coherence and the well-functioning of global markets, in addition to others. Although growth-focused collaboration at the international level can help progress in many areas, this needs to be complemented by collaboration in the sustainability and social areas in particular.

Further analysis of policies which impact these issues is needed

Further headway needs to be made in policy analysis across a number of areas, including the innovation framework and the measurement of sustainable productivity within the context of Green Growth. The improvement of policy measurement and evaluation is also necessary as a basis for robust strategies.

Chapter 1

Key trends and long-term scenarios: Framing the future of food and agriculture

Three key trends currently frame the future challenges facing our food and agriculture systems: growing and shifting food demand, constraints upon natural resources, and agricultural productivity uncertainties resulting from climate change. The choices made by policy makers and businesses today will be pivotal in determining the extent to which global food and agriculture systems will be impacted by these trials. Nevertheless, the uncertainties which surround future challenges pose substantial obstacles to the formulation of policy and industry strategies that will be effective across a range of scenarios in the long run. While scenario analysis does not present "forecasts" and is subject to numerous caveats, it can provide a useful alternative approach to dealing with an inherently uncertain future. This chapter presents three long-term scenarios for the world in 2050 – Individual, Fossil Fuel-Driven Growth; Citizen-Driven, Sustainable Growth; and Fast, Globally-Driven Growth – and explores the agricultural markets within these alternative "futures".

Framing the future of food and agriculture

The current debate on food and agriculture: Why should we worry?

The global food system will face a formidable array of challenges over the coming decades. Not only must it produce increasing volumes of food for a growing and more affluent population that demands a more diverse diet, it must also – in many developing countries in particular – contribute to economic growth, poverty alleviation, rural employment and development.[1] Added to this, agricultural systems must face increased competition for alternative uses of increasingly limited natural resources such as land and water, while helping to preserve biodiversity, restoring fragile ecosystems and contributing to climate change mitigation. Finally, farmers will also have to adapt to the unpredictable effects of climate change, including higher average temperatures and more frequent extreme weather events, such as temperature peaks, droughts and floods which worsen the risks to food security. The impacts of these challenges, and of efforts by agricultural and food chain actors to address these, will in turn affect societies and economies on multiple wider levels.

Key trends in 2015

Three key trends currently frame the abovementioned challenges facing food and agriculture: growing and shifting food demand, constraints upon natural resources, and agricultural productivity uncertainties resulting from climate change.

Growing and shifting food demand

Demand for agricultural produce will continue to grow, driven by population growth and increasing incomes. Global population growth rates peaked in the mid-1980s and have been declining ever since, yet remain at about 1.2% per year, with little change over the first decade of the 21st century. Each year alone, the world population increases by more than 80 million. The majority of population growth occurs within emerging economies – the population of India currently adds 15 million per year to the world total – and developing countries: with 2.5% and a further 25 million people per year, Africa is the continent with the fastest-growing population. In contrast, however, population growth in most OECD countries today is small or even negative. As a consequence, while global food demand is growing, it is also *shifting* towards the developing world.

Significant progress has certainly been made towards achieving the Millennium Development Goal of halving the share of undernourished people in developing countries by 2015. Nevertheless, this progress has been regionally uneven, and the number of hungry worldwide remains unacceptably high, at over 800 million (FAO, 2014a). Whereas India and the People's Republic of China (hereafter "China") represent the largest undernourished populations, Sub-Saharan Africa remains the region where hunger is most prevalent. At the same time, overweight and obesity have become major concerns within OECD and rapidly-developing transition economies (OECD, 2013a; WHO, 2015).

Global GDP grew by circa 3.8% per year in real terms between 2002 and 2011, with the OECD economy growing much more slowly than the non-OECD area (1.7% per annum compared to 7.1% per annum, respectively; OECD, 2014b). In other words, while average real per capita incomes within the OECD increased by just 1% a year, they rose by some 5.7% elsewhere. Although these figures have mostly been lower in recent years, and will certainly change in the future, a continued convergence of per capita income levels is expected which will contribute to the shift in global food demand towards emerging and developing countries. The significant increase in per capita incomes outside the OECD area in particular also suggests a continued shift in global consumption patterns in favour of diets that are richer – not only in animal protein and sugar, but also in fruits and vegetables. Such a shift is likely to improve the nutritional status and health of many of today's poor, who otherwise base their diets largely on staple crops. Nevertheless, it will also increase demand for land and other resources which are necessary for agricultural production.

Constraints on natural resources

Agricultural land expansion has slowed down globally and is largely limited to Latin America and Africa. Globally, agricultural land use in 2008-12 was 10% or 440 million ha larger than during 1961-65, yet practically all of this net growth occurred before the mid-1990s (FAOSTAT, 2014). South America and Africa account for almost two-thirds of the total increase. While there are a range of studies which suggest that significant additional land could be suitable for agricultural production (see Foresight, 2011, for a more detailed discussion), agricultural expansion faces a number of economic and environmental challenges. Soil degradation, for example, adds to constraints related to available productive land, originating in desertification, salinisation, erosion and loss of soil carbon, and other factors frequently linked to agricultural production (see GLASOD, 1990; Eswaran et al., 2001).

Historically, land use change and the conversion of habitat to other land uses, notably for agricultural production, is a main driver of biodiversity loss, together with pollution, overexploitation of natural resources by overfishing or overhunting, for example, invasive alien species and, increasingly, climate change (Slingenberg et al., 2009; OECD, 2012). Global forest cover has declined by some 3.4% between 1990 and 2010 (OECD, 2012). Primary forests, which represent about 36% of the total and which tend to be particularly biodiversity-rich, have shrunk twice as fast as total forest over the last two decades.

Biodiversity,[2] and the ecosystems of which the range of organisms are part, provide important – although largely unvalued – services to both human populations and the environment. At a global level, as well as in most regions, biodiversity has been declining for decades.[3] The abundance of vertebrate animals and other species declined between 1970 and 2010: about 11% and 30% respectively have been lost, with significant variability across regions and habitats (OECD, 2012). Marine biodiversity has also become increasingly endangered following the progressive over-exploitation of marine fish stocks in recent decades. Today, the share of over-exploited fish stocks is above 30%, while under 20% of stocks are less than fully exploited.

Agriculture accounts for some 70% of global freshwater withdrawals, with higher shares in many developing countries. Over the past century, global water demand has increased about twice as fast as total population, even though freshwater abstraction within the OECD area has not increased since 1990 (OECD, 2012). Water is probably abundant at a global scale, however a large number of countries face increasingly severe water shortages during growing seasons. Severe water stress has been identified for large regions in southern North America, Mediterranean Europe, South Africa and the southern half of Asia, and estimates suggest that water stress will become more widespread in the decades to come (op. cit.). Given the importance of water supplies for agricultural production, this may have substantial implications for food markets. In addition to the availability of sufficient fresh-water volumes, water quality is increasingly threatened by nutrient runoffs and poor wastewater treatment outside the OECD in particular, as well as by a range of micro-pollutants.

Raw materials for basic fertilisers, such as phosphorus and potash, are concentrated within a limited number of countries and have been discussed as non-renewable and scarce resources by some (e.g. Cordell et al., 2009; Grantham, 2011). Production of potash is limited to 17 countries, with Canada, Russian Federation and Belarus accounting for almost two-thirds of global supply in 2012 (FAOSTAT, 2014). However, this does not imply short supplies in the future, and a few other countries, such as the Republic of Congo, may develop additional production potential (Mineweb, 2013). It is estimated that global reserves of up to 16 billion tonnes of K_2O are minable with current technologies (Kali and Salz, undated), some 500 times the average annual volume produced during 2008-2012. On the other hand, the vast majority of countries entirely depend on imports for this essential crop nutrient. To a lesser degree, this also holds for phosphorus, for which the FAO reports 59 producing countries in 2012, and for which economically exploitable reserves are estimated at 18 billion tonnes (Elsner, 2008), or some 370 times the current annual production (average of 2002-2012, calculated from FAOSTAT, 2014, and Elsner, 2008).

Future fossil fuel resources for agricultural and process energy requirements are considered to be uncertain in the longer run. This concern may have decreased somewhat, due to the recent drop in energy and, more specifically, crude oil prices. Nonetheless, the International Energy Agency notes rising unease regarding energy security in the medium and longer term (IEA, 2014), linked to fast-growing energy demand in emerging and developing countries and persistent uncertainties regarding Middle East developments. Given the importance of energy for agricultural production costs – related both to energy as a direct input in agricultural production and as a driver for other input markets, such as fertilisers and chemicals – and the increased use of agricultural biomass for fuel generation, such uncertainty is likely to be transmitted into food and agriculture systems in future.

Agricultural productivity uncertainties resulting from climate change

Greenhouse gas (GHG) concentrations in the global atmosphere have increased substantially over the past 200 years, with significant acceleration since the 1950s. Concentrations of carbon dioxide (CO_2), methane (CH_4) and nitrous oxide (N_2O) have increased by 40%, 150% and 20% since 1750, respectively (IPCC, 2013). Anthropogenic factors significantly exceed natural drivers in their effects on radiative forcing, which is estimated to have increased by around 2.3 Watt per m^2 since 1750. The majority of this increase is due to emissions related to fossil fuel combustion, cement production and flaring, while land use-related emissions have also been significant. Annual anthropogenic GHG emissions have increased by about 80% between 1970 and 2010. Roughly one-fourth of these emissions in 2010 were related to agriculture, forestry and other land use.

As a result of these growing GHG concentrations, global surface temperatures have been steadily increasing. The last three decades have been "successively warmer at the Earth's surface than any preceding decade since 1850," with an estimated warming of 0.85°C since 1880. Meanwhile, an increase in extreme events related to high temperature as well as heavy precipitation events in a number of regions have been linked to human influences (IPCC, 2013).

Evidence from the available literature suggests that climate change has already had measurable implications for the physical (e.g. glaciers, coastal erosion), biological (e.g. ecosystems, wildfires) and human and managed systems (e.g. food production, health) (IPCC, 2014). However, the extent to which global temperatures will change in the future, the consequences that this will have for the regional and temporal distribution of temperature and precipitation, and hence the implications for agricultural productivity, are all subject to significant uncertainty. Numerous research efforts are underway to shed light on the complex relationships between emissions, the atmospheric content of greenhouse gases, surface temperatures, precipitation, crop and livestock productivity, and agricultural markets. It seems increasingly likely, however, that without greater efforts to combat climate change and mitigate its negative effects, stronger economic growth – a key driver to improving the fate of billions of poor people – will likely increase greenhouse gas emissions and hence negatively affect the productive capacity of the agricultural sector, particularly in developing countries.

Scenarios as a tool to explore possible futures

The choices made by policy makers and businesses today will be pivotal in determining the extent to which global food and agriculture systems will be impacted by the abovementioned challenges. Nevertheless, the *uncertainties* which surround these challenges pose substantial obstacles to the formulation of policy and industry strategies that will be effective across a range of scenarios in the long run. Unsurprisingly, these uncertainties become more significant as the time horizon is extended farther into the future. Projections or forecasts for markets are, by design, based on past information, and are of limited use when responses to systemic uncertainties that unfold over a longer time horizon are explored.

There are a number of ongoing activities which discuss expected short- and medium-term developments on global agricultural markets, including the bi-annual *FAO Food Outlook* (FAO, 2014b), the (quasi-)monthly AMIS Market Monitor (AMIS, 2015), the annual *OECD-FAO Agricultural Outlook* (OECD/FAO, 2014) and others. While the medium-term Agricultural Outlook provides projections based on a number of – in parts quite stringent – assumptions rather than forecasts, such projections are subject to substantial uncertainties and, as a consequence, are revised on an annual basis.

Scenario analysis provides an alternative approach to dealing with an inherently uncertain future. While they do not represent "forecasts" or "projections", and are also subject to numerous caveats and uncertainties, which are outlined below, scenarios provide a tool for the consideration of different possible futures, taking political, economic, technological and other "known unknowns" into account. Both in the form of qualitative storylines and as quantitative, model-driven pathways for relevant variables, scenarios explicitly account for the uncertainties which can frequently burden the policy discussion: relevant drivers may follow different paths, the links between these drivers and target variables, as well as their future development, is subject to partial information only, and the interpretation of outcomes is often subjective.

The consideration of several alternative "futures", which emphasise the different challenges to varying degrees, can facilitate the discussion and questioning of pre-existing assumptions on the development of, and linkages between, different drivers and outcomes. Debates such as these are a necessary foundation for the re-thinking of strategies with a view to the development of coherent, robust policy and private sector responses to avail of new opportunities and avoid more of the undesired outcomes – whatever the state of the world in the future.

Nevertheless, the scenario analysis undertaken for this report necessarily remains incomplete and subject to a number of limitations which need to be borne in mind. Firstly, as the development and analysis of the scenario has predominantly involved government officials, it underrepresents the views of other stakeholders. Secondly, the quantification of certain aspects of the scenarios excludes other elements which are relevant for the discussion and, as is the case with other modelling work, represents a partial and simplified view of the issues at hand. In particular, questions related to instabilities or to the heterogeneity within societies and farm sectors, the structure of value chains, and to market volatility and shocks, tend to be hidden in the deterministic and averaging nature of the model outcomes, and were only partly covered by the workshop discussions. In addition, the uncertainties involved in estimating the speed of key variables, such as productivity growth, remain a challenge for model-supported foresight work.

Finally, while the quantification of the scenarios is based on existing and well-established work in the field, the results show substantial variability across the four economic models employed. This range of outcomes is not a flaw of the approach taken – it is a reality inherent in our highly uncertain future. This strengthens the argument for continued foresight efforts to identify possible risks and opportunities so that policy actions can be taken early to increase positive outcomes while mitigating the negative ones.

The three OECD long-term scenarios for food and agriculture presented within this study relate to, and partly build upon, a number of related foresight and scenario activities (Box 1.1). This report complements other work through the strong involvement of agricultural Ministries within OECD member countries (as well as some emerging economies), which outlined the different scenarios, discussed their implications and developed strategies to overcome some of the major challenges for future food and agriculture systems.

Box 1.1. OECD scenarios within the context of other scenario activities

The OECD Long-Term Scenarios for Food and Agriculture project complements other related scenario work. As a co-operative effort involving a large number of researchers, the International Panel on Climate Change has developed a set of shared socio-economic pathways (SSPs, see IPCC, 2014), which were originally intended to serve the work on climate change but which also form a key input to several other scenario activities, including the OECD scenarios. Earlier work by the IPCC includes the Special Report on Emissions Scenarios (SRES, see IPCC, 2000), which focuses on the quantification of emissions and is mainly used in the Third and Fourth IPCC Assessment Reports.

The United Nations-based *Millennium Ecosystem Assessment* (2005) includes four contrasting global scenarios which aim to "assess the consequences of ecosystem change for human well-being and to establish the scientific basis for actions needed to enhance the conservation and sustainable use of ecosystems" (op.cit.: ii).

Earthscan and the International Water Management Institute's *Comprehensive Assessment of Water Management in Agriculture* (2007) aims at "assessing the current state of knowledge and stimulating ideas on how to manage water resources to meet the growing needs for agricultural products, to help reduce poverty and food insecurity, and to contribute to environmental sustainability" (op.cit.:v), and includes a baseline and six different scenarios on water use in agriculture.

The *International Assessment of Agricultural Knowledge, Science and Technology for Development* (UNEP, 2009), initiated by the World Bank and the FAO, aims to assess the "impacts of past, present and future agricultural knowledge, science and technology on the reduction of hunger and poverty, improvement of rural livelihoods and human health, and equitable, socially, environmentally and economically sustainable development (op.cit. p. vi). Its scenario analysis includes a baseline and four different policy experiments.

Agrimonde is a joint foresight activity by the French research institutes INRA and CIRAD (Dorin et al., 2011). It aims to produce "scenarios of global and regional evolution in agricultural production, consumption and trade, as well as in scientific and technical knowledge on agriculture, with a view to drawing conclusions on the possible roles for research, public policies and international regulations" (summary report, p. 2), and includes a trend-based reference scenario as well as a normative Agrimonde 1 scenario.

The European-funded FoodSecure project (www.FoodSecure.eu) aims to design "effective and sustainable strategies for assessing and addressing the challenges of food and nutrition security". Its Work Package 5 involves the development of a set of scenarios by stakeholders, the definition of a desired future for food and nutrition security ("vision"), and the identification of suitable policy options to come closer to that "vision".

A number of other institutions have engaged in global scenarios for or related to agriculture, including the International Food Policy Research Institute (e.g. Nelson et al., 2010), the UN Food and Agriculture Organization (e.g. Alexandratos and Bruinsmaa, 2012), and the United Nations Environmental Programme (UNEP, 2012). The UK Foresight's *The Future of Food and Farming* (www.bis.gov.uk/foresight/our-work/projects/published-projects/global-food-and-farming-futures) also explores "the increasing pressures on the global food system between now and 2050" (Foresight, 2011).

At regional and local levels, the research programme on Climate Change, Agriculture and Food Security (https://ccafs.cgiar.org), funded by government and aid agencies and linked to the Consultative Group on International Agricultural Research (CGIAR), is a foresight-based programme to develop policy and investment options to promote climate-smart and sustainable agricultural practices in Latin America, Sub-Saharan Africa and South and Southeast Asia. Similarly, the Global Futures and Strategic Foresight project, also within CGIAR, is designed "to improve agricultural productivity and environmental sustainability, especially in developing countries" (www.globalfutures.cgiar.org). Other scenario work relates more directly to water: the Water Futures and Solutions – World Water Scenarios partnership between the International Institute for Applied Systems Analysis (IIASA), the International Water Association (IWA), the World Water Council (WWC), UNESCO and the Korean Government (www.iiasa.ac.at/web/home/research/wfas-summary.html), for example.

Further information on several of the abovementioned scenario activities can be found in van Dijk and Meijerink (2014).

Critical drivers for food and agriculture towards 2050

Basic dimensions of the OECD long-term scenarios for food and agriculture

The design of scenarios (see Box 1.2 for a brief description of the approach used in this work) begins with the identification of the dimensions that together establish the context in which the narratives are developed, and define the broad scope in which the subsequent qualitative and quantitative analysis is carried out. Three main dimensions characterise the different scenarios defined in this report. These dimensions, which are briefly outlined below, cover: the scope and depth of international co-operation; technological innovation and diffusion pathways; and the development of sustainable mindsets across societies.

Box 1.2. The approach and methodology for generating and analysing the OECD long-term scenarios

This work was structured around two two-day workshops. In each workshop, about 60 participants – officials from OECD and non-member ministries responsible for food and agriculture, subject matter experts and economic modellers in particular – participated in the development and discussion of the three scenarios, their implications for food and agriculture, and response strategies for improving the outcomes. The first workshop, "Storylines, challenges and policy opportunities", considered and mapped the complexity of issues and the uncertainties that characterise the development of food systems' security and sustainability over the coming decades, from different stakeholder perspectives. It included the co-development and agreement on three scenario frames and basic storylines relevant to food and agriculture towards the middle of this century. These were used for a first identification of threats and opportunities arising from the scenarios, and to explore fundamental options for more robust policy making.

Following the completion of the scenario storylines by the core project team, the scenarios were quantified with the help of several global economic models. The model outcomes allowed the challenges and opportunities identified by workshop participants to be illustrated with numbers, and informed the discussions during the second workshop.

The second workshop, "Robust policy choices for the coming decades", subsequently facilitated an open exchange across countries and, to a more limited extent, between governments, industry and civil society. It addressed and evaluated public and private responses to the challenges and opportunities for food and agriculture, and enabled the development of a shared view on best common strategies to improve the resilience and preparedness of agriculture and food systems.

Both workshops were structured to maximise participant interaction in an outcome-orientated manner. The majority of the conversation took place within different forms of break-out sessions featuring small groups. Plenary presentations were largely limited to concise introductions to open the debate, *carousel* processes enabled participants to join a selection of specific issues consecutively, a recap session at the start of the second workshop allowed participants to (re-)familiarise themselves with the scenarios and their basic outcomes, and a coffee house-style market for ideas provided opportunities for a collection of participants' proposals for short- and medium-term action.

In addition to the results from the economic models, which provided quantitative analysis of some of the scenario implications for food and agriculture, a range of other inputs provided the background for the discussions at the second workshop. These included: i) a set of "scenario posters" as concise communication tools that supported participants in their rapid (re-)familiarisation with storylines and key characteristics of the different scenarios. Similar posters were also prepared to introduce other specific elements of relevance for the workshop conversations, such as information on the important area of fisheries (both caught fish and aquaculture); and ii) a range of complementary working notes on themes for which quantification by the economic models was not (sufficiently) possible, which were provided by subject matter experts. These notes covered fisheries and aquaculture; extreme events and agricultural insurance; trans-boundary livestock diseases; agriculture, biodiversity and sustainable development; the future of food consumption; and agricultural risk management systems. A substantial proportion of these notes informed the writing of this report.

Between and after the workshops, a dedicated electronic discussion forum, accessible to all workshop participants, enabled further exchange and comments, in addition to the sharing of background material well in advance of the second workshop. The forum also aims to facilitate continued conversation among participants beyond the lifespan of the original two-year project. Securing the engagement of government officials and other participants, and opportunities for intense conversations and networking at, between and after the workshops, are necessary to ensure that participants and countries identify with the scenarios and their implications.

The use of the scenarios for foresight-based policy discussions and the availability of a space for constructive disagreements continue to be of key importance for the OECD work on long-term scenarios for food and agriculture.

Scope and depth of international co-operation

This dimension is based on the following relatively profound question: How will individual countries and country groups co-operate with each other in future? Regional and global co-operation is not confined to regional or international trade agreements, but also includes exchanges and collaboration across various economic, societal, environmental and political levels more generally. Co-operation may either take place on an *ad hoc* basis, or be grounded in specific or more general agreements which may be of a more or less permanent nature. Although the concept of co-operation is closely related to the question of governance, it in fact extends beyond governmental collaboration to include the role of private companies and other actors.

Technological innovation and diffusion pathways

What will be the main orientation of future developments in technologies, production methods, knowledge exchange, etc.? To what degree will the focus be on reducing the environmental and social footprint of production processes? Will new technologies be available to large parts of the world population (the poorest), or will technology divides increase? While this dimension is to some extent related to the sustainable mindsets and international co-operation dimensions, it also takes scientific developments and the dynamics of innovation systems into account

Development of sustainable mindsets

How will consumer and citizen attitudes towards sustainable behaviour develop over the coming decades? These attitudes include consumption patterns with respect to products and services, but equally concern developments towards the provision of public goods – and the avoidance of public "bads". A more sustainable mindset might, for example, result in stronger demand for specific food and nutrition goals to be included within the global sustainable development agenda.

The three dimensions are not mutually exclusive, and in fact tend to influence each other. An additional, over-arching aspect relates to the stability of political, economic and social systems and their ability to cope with external shocks. Resilience will clearly be influenced by factors related to international co-operation, technological developments and societies' focus on sustainable systems.

Alternative views of the world in 2050: The OECD long-term scenarios

Three broad, contrasting scenarios were identified. Their purpose is not to predict but to highlight the fundamental uncertainties that surround forward-oriented decision making. Each of these depict the potential future of global food and agriculture in different ways:

- The **Individual, Fossil Fuel-Driven Growth** scenario illustrates a world which is driven by sovereignty and self-sufficiency, characterised by the strong focus of individual regions on economic growth based on fossil energy sources and related technologies, and relatively minimal emphasis by governments or their citizens on environmental or social questions. Co-operation is limited to regional alliances, both ad hoc and more durable, and is driven by national interests rather than long-term geo-political visions. Technological developments focus on fossil fuel extraction.
- The **Citizen-Driven, Sustainable Growth** scenario portrays a world in which individual countries push for the more sustainable development of their economies, driven mainly by changes in the attitudes of consumers and citizens. Global co-operation is relatively limited. Technologies are focused on natural resource savings and the preservation of the environment.
- The **Fast, Globally-Driven Growth** scenario represents a world that is characterised by a strong focus on international co-operation with the aim of fostering economic growth and prosperity.

Markets and large companies play key roles in the rapid economic development, while environmental issues receive less attention from governments or their citizens. Technologies flourish, particularly in the areas of food, feed and energy production.

Individual, Fossil Fuel-Driven Growth: A world of sovereignty and self-sufficiency ambitions

The **Individual, Fossil Fuel-Driven Growth** scenario (or the "*Individual*" scenario in short) develops in response to experiences of the reduced reliability of global governance structures – long and only partially successful negotiations for multilateral agreements on trade, carbon emissions, etc. – and a move towards more *regional* collaboration. It is characterised by a strong focus of individual regions on economic growth, making use of different options to overcome scarcities of energy and other natural resources. Technological developments focus on the efficient extraction of fossil energy sources where these are available, e.g. shale gas, coal conversion and deep-sea off-shore oil wells, while bioenergy is seen as a solution by regions that are energy resource-constrained but relatively abundant in land. Markets are developed by resource-rich countries in regional trading blocs with populous countries (e.g. the Russian Federation with China, but co-operation is driven by national interests rather than long-term geo-political visions, and is partly sector-specific. Global value chains (GVCs) are increasingly replaced (or, at least, complemented) by regional value chains (RVCs). Technological spill-overs, strongly related to trade in intermediate inputs, tend to be much stronger at regional level than at global level.

Continued political instability in vulnerable regions, such as the Middle East and parts of Africa, is another characteristic of this scenario. Here, economic and societal developments remain much slower than elsewhere, following reduced investments, smaller trade integration, lack of infrastructure, etc. In many parts of the world, however, investments in technologies based on fossil fuels and other natural resources, related research and development, and reasonable trade growth within regional blocks create significant income growth, although inequalities both across and within countries tend to increase. National governments play a key role in defending the interests of country populations.

In the *Individual* scenario, relatively strong population growth and increased urbanisation increase pressures on food markets. While average incomes continue to grow around the globe, inequalities increase across and within regions and countries. Energy availability is not a significant problem and is very much focused upon fossil sources. Scarcities in the supply of water and other natural resources, in contrast, continue to worsen in many regions following largely uncontrolled use. In line with developments in other fossil resource-based sectors, agricultural productivity increases strongly, thus partly offsetting the negative impacts of scarce resources on overall supply.

Greenhouse gas (GHG) emissions continue to rise significantly as a consequence of the focus on fossil resources and of little environmental consciousness in consumer choice in many parts of the world. GHG emissions are dampened only by the moderate growth of many economies. Overall, this moderately high emission pathway has negative consequences for the climate.

The agricultural system is highly input-intensive and based on high productivity. Production systems in rural agriculture converge towards large-scale, technology-oriented systems with little emphasis on environmental problems unless these have direct and measurable consequences for agricultural production. Biodiversity losses within agricultural biosystems are generally compensated for by technological developments and farming practices that allow the efficient conversion of plant and feed nutrients into crop and animal yields.

Strategies and policy mixes which promote high levels of independence from inter-regional food imports are quite different across the large regions and even across countries *within* these regions. Like other sectors, agriculture is heavily reliant on fossil energies, although region-specific biofuel options might generate some flexibility within the system. Agricultural food production is complemented by on-land or on-shore aquaculture, which partly competes for the same resources. International trade between regions in particular is low, and international co-operation is generally less intense. Hence, differences in resource endowments, climate change impacts and other factors driving comparative advantages result in relatively strong differences in agricultural and food supplies and thus diverging prices between regions.

With rising per capita incomes in most regions of the world, consumers continue to increase their demand for protein-rich and animal product-based diets, with little attention given to environmental, social or other characteristics which are not immediately visible from the product. Consumption also moves towards increased levels of processing, in combination with added services (away-from-home consumption, deliveries, ready-to-consume products). As a consequence, regional value chains and distances travelled by food products, while remaining largely within regional boundaries, can be long.

Citizen-Driven, Sustainable Growth: A world of environmental and social focus

The **Citizen-Driven, Sustainable Growth** scenario (or the "*Sustainable*" scenario in short) is founded on a strongly developing mindset of consumers and citizens in favour of sustainable consumption and development. The majority of the population put increased emphasis on how the goods they consume are produced, and consider their environmental and social footprint for everyday decisions. They also engage in orienting policies towards low-carbon transport systems and sustainable urban development, although specific views on what constitutes "sustainable development" differ across countries and regions. As a consequence, global co-operation is much more limited, and individual countries develop their own strategies to make their economies greener, while neighbouring countries with similar conditions follow by adopting these strategies. These strategies can differ substantially between large regions, and co-operation is largely limited to the exchange and harmonisation of systems within them. National governments play a key role in building regional coalitions. At the same time, civil society organisations are pivotal in driving the respective sustainability agendas within their regions.

As a result, the majority of research and development efforts are focused on natural resource savings and environment preservation. Methods and technologies, while relatively easily shared within regions, remain segregated across regions. Within countries and regions, enhanced social engagement improves access to resources (food, wealth, education, technologies etc.) for all segments of society. Despite lower GHG emissions and hence reduced risks of climate change-related shocks, the lack of developed global infrastructure (trade, regulations, cultural co-operation, languages etc.) increases vulnerability with respect to political and economic shocks.

There is a development away from global towards regional value chains. Where regional coalitions are sufficiently large, this does not reduce the efficiency of these value chains, however changing coalitions increase the risk of disruptions.

The *Sustainable* scenario is also characterised by substantial social awareness and efforts towards more cohesive societies. This results in high and widespread education as well as reduced population growth, while a general interest in a "green" life – notably in developed countries – slows down and partly reverses the urbanisation process. Wealthy consumers, in high-income countries in particular, show an increasing interest in more healthy and less meat-based diets, although income and population growth in low- and middle-income countries continues to raise meat consumption in these regions. Higher education levels and high R&D also allow for fast and variable input-saving productivity growth in agriculture and in other sectors. Nonetheless, land productivity on average suffers from input constraints imposed by consumers and civil society. Income growth is dampened by a lack of global co-operation but benefits from productivity growth and the availability of skilled labour.

While fossil energy reserves are shrinking, and those remaining sources face substantial carbon taxation in a number of countries, renewable energy sources are developing rapidly, providing sufficient and fairly economic supplies, and the significantly reduced energy dependency of economies leads to declining energy demand overall. Other natural resources, such as water, experience similar deceleration in demand due to their more efficient use. On the other hand, local tensions may arise between food and non-food uses – renewable energy included – of biomass and related production factors.

Climate change, while continuing, slows down significantly due to substantial reductions in GHG emissions. The increase of global average surface temperatures is limited to 2-3 degrees, which in higher latitudes further improves agricultural yields without dramatic negative impacts in lower latitudes. The world follows a relatively low emission pathway.

Due to these drivers, the agricultural system features productivity gains which focus mainly on reducing overall input use, such as water, fertilisers, pesticide agents, etc. Many consumers, in the developed world in particular, redirect their demand in favour of food from environment-friendly production methods, accepting the higher prices resulting from the relatively lower yields that are related to such production. Natural reserves, rural settlements and infrastructure tend to reduce the land base used for agricultural production, notably in developed countries. Environmental priorities characterise the far-reaching consensus between farming, processing and retail sectors and food consumers, with green growth becoming increasingly mainstream. The lower intake of livestock products, in high-income countries in particular, compared to other scenarios; the stronger reliance on plant-based protein; and increased efforts to reduce food waste along the supply chain all tend to reduce pressures on agricultural and food markets.

Agriculture also increasingly provides bio-based raw materials for a range of products other than food. With the re-use of waste materials, overall demand for agricultural materials remains, however, lower than what the replacement of formerly fossil-based materials would otherwise suggest. Off-shore aquaculture adds to food supplies; however, due to the lack of global agreement on the sustainable exploitation of the sea, its contribution is limited. At the same time, urban food production, favoured by the increased attention to food miles and shorter supply chains, is limited by citizens' demand for green space within cities. An increased focus is put on connecting cities and rural areas, resulting in the increased importance of peri-urban supply chains.

Fast, Globally-Driven Growth: A world of co-operative economic growth

The **Fast, Globally-Driven Growth** scenario (or the "Fast" scenario in short) is driven by a revival of multilateralism, supported by the growth engines of China and India, as well as Brazil and other South Asian economies. In spite of some progress made within climate change negotiations, such as the COP21 Conference in Paris in December 2015, and a general commitment to increasing the carbon efficiencies of economic growth, growing economies continue to increase their emissions. However, a strong focus on multilateral co-operation in international trade leads to a far-reaching global trade agreement facilitated by the WTO. International co-operation is also a strong driver for international corporations. It facilitates the innovation process and efficient supply chains, and reinforces the market power of large multinationals. Rapidly developing new technologies and production methods for food, feed and energy help to accommodate the needs of the significantly increasing global population and cope with looming resource scarcities. Flourishing developments include hydrogen and fuel cells, battery vehicles, biofuels, green chemistry, remote sensing and other technologies. With less oversight by nation states, global economic prospects are for close to 4% annual growth of per capita GDP for a 20-year period. Rapid urbanisation and the accelerated development of mega-poles are meanwhile spreading across the globe, with little attention given to food diversity, biodiversity or cultural diversity. CEOs of multinationals and mayors of mega-poles have significant influence over key decisions and are potentially more influential than national governments or inter-governmental organisations.

Global trade quadruples by 2030, and food production increases rapidly. Not everyone wins, however, and discrepancies are significant. Income and wealth inequalities between countries and individuals rise. Even if Sub-Saharan Africa has consistently reached a positive growth rate over the period, access to basic resources such as food, water, shelters and education is still an issue for a significant proportion of the population. As was the case in the early 2000s, certain commodities or rare materials shortages and sectoral trade wars can be frequent, due to transitions in consumption patterns, bad crops, or low stocks. Europe, the Americas and the Black Sea region maintain their position as the backbone of stable agricultural production and to a certain extent provide a safety net for the rest of the world.

Strong globalisation, rapid urbanisation, highly engineered infrastructure and high investment in technological innovation lead to very resource-intensive land use in agriculture, increased input in the form of fertilisers, highly managed agro-ecosystems and meat-rich diets. However, a dual system of agriculture can be observed, with smaller multifunctional farms flourishing at the same time as the intensive large scale farms which are highly integrated within the global supply chain. Well-educated farmers embrace new production methods and technologies in both categories.

Thanks to technological developments as well as biomass-based sources, energy remains relatively cheap. As a consequence, productivity of land, labour and capital use in agriculture and food manufacturing is very high, favouring large international trade flows and global markets. This results in the larger choice of food products within countries at the expense of diversity in global food consumption patterns.

As a result of the rapidly growing global population and rising incomes, consumption growth of food and energy is very high in certain regions, Sub-Saharan Africa, Southeast Asia and some Latin American countries included. Strong economic growth results in a further strong increase in GHG emissions, with severe consequences for the climate – even if the carbon intensity of many economies is not extremely high. The world therefore follows a high emission pathway. Water remains an issue within some parts of the world, as climate change exacerbates drought and competition, while human consumption takes a larger share of available water away from the agricultural sector. In addition, the agricultural system has to bear with land losses in coastal areas due to rising sea levels, and in arid areas due to desertification.

The majority of the agricultural system is highly managed, with a strong level of integration along the value chain. The lion's share of agricultural production is resource and land use-intensive. Markets and downstream industries, such as brokers, multinationals and retailers, wield strong influence over structural changes, and food supply chains tend to be long, with significant specialisation between firms and countries. As a consequence, productivity gains are rapid and widely spread. New technologies are shared quickly and partly provided to farmers via the integrated supply chain. A small segment of multi-functional farms help to serve the niche markets of wealthier consumers. In parallel, expanding urban areas develop new agricultural production systems that become increasingly soil-independent. Plant nutrients, technical CO_2 fertilisation and artificial light are converted into biomass in industrial and largely automated production towers, providing vegetables and other products for urban customers. In turn, however, a large number of marginal and subsistence farmers in developing countries may see themselves left behind and without the required links to value chains and consumer markets.

Some systemic risks are reinforced through market concentration, with a few large multi-national firms potentially exercising important market power. Similarly, the growing importance of the e-economy within the food and agriculture sector increases the potential vulnerability to technical risks.

Off-shore aquaculture provides significant quantities of fish, based on technological developments, strong co-operation and international agreements on the exploitation of the off-shore sea. This is, however, a development with peaks and troughs, as fish diseases repeatedly disrupt the systems.

There is a strong push for various forms of bioenergy and other bio-based products. Access to resources, land and water in particular, is unequally distributed across countries and affected by climate change impacts. At the same time, however, international co-operation enables the development of large-scale off-shore aquaculture, contributing to food supplies from land-based production systems. International trade expands under the influence of a general tendency towards more open markets and the enlarged role of e-commerce platforms, linking companies of all sizes more or less directly to their consumers abroad. As a result, compensation can take place between countries and regions in the event of local shortages, such as drought in South Asia, or price hikes, to smoothen the potential negative impacts of such shocks.

Key prospects for agricultural markets within the scenarios

Given these differing characteristics, what then are the implications for agricultural markets within these alternative futures? Simulations with four global economic models show that the prospects for agricultural production and farm incomes vary around the historical trends, driven by the assumptions embedded in the scenarios (see Box 1.3 for a brief presentation of how the scenarios were quantified). A major shift in agricultural prices is visible, however. The evolution of food demand is chief amongst the driving factors, together with agricultural productivity growth and the expansion of the cultivated land.

Box 1.3. Quantifying the OECD long-term scenarios

To quantify key aspects of the OECD scenarios and the implications of those scenarios and of different policy strategies for some of the main outcomes in food and agriculture, four global economic models with a focus on this sector have been used. These include two computable general-equilibrium (CGE) models: the ENVISAGE model originally developed and applied by the World Bank, designed specifically to analyse climate change issues, and the MAGNET model developed and applied by LEI, part of Wageningen-UR, focusing among others on agricultural policies, land use and productivity questions. Two partial-equilibrium models were also used: the IIASA's GLOBIOM model, developed mainly for the assessment of climate change mitigation policies in land-based sectors, and IFPRI's IMPACT model, focusing on the linkages between agricultural production and national food security. More details on these models and related references can be found in Annex 1.A1.

Quantifying the OECD scenarios with the help of the four economic models requires the detailed specification of a range of key drivers used as exogenous variables in the models. These drivers relate to demographic and macroeconomic developments (population growth, developments in per capita GDP), agricultural productivity growth (exogenous or "intrinsic growth" in crop and grassland yields, feed conversion efficiencies), the yield-reducing effects of climate change for crops and grassland, energy – and, hence, fertiliser – prices, assumptions on structural changes in food demand patterns, and general assumptions on policy developments, e.g. on biofuel support and on food trade costs related to regulatory differences. To the degree possible, the quantification of these drivers is based on previous scenario work, notably in the context of climate change research: each of the three scenarios is loosely linked to one of the IPCC's (Intergovernmental Panel on Climate Change) shared socio-economic pathways (SSPs), while the qualitative implications for climate change are translated into one of the representative concentration pathways (RCPs) also developed in the context of the IPCC work. Other existing projections used include work by the International Food Policy Research Institute (IFPRI) on crop productivity; work on productivity growth in grassland and feed conversion efficiency growth by the Netherlands Environmental Assessment Agency PBL; the International Energy Agency (IEA) Current Policy Scenario both for energy prices; and, for the Citizen-Driven, Sustainable Growth scenario, ongoing work by the International Institute for Applied Systems Analysis (IIASA) on sustainable diets. The three scenario storylines are presented in greater detail in the Annex to this chapter, and more information on the specific SSPs and RCPs chosen and the specific adjustments made to better reflect these qualitative storylines can be found in Annex 1.A2. Key differences in the drivers across the three scenarios need to be highlighted to facilitate the reading of the quantitative scenario results presented in this report.

Box 1.3. Quantifying the OECD long-term scenarios *(continued)*

Quantification of the **Individual, Fossil Fuel-Driven Growth** scenario is driven by the highest population growth, reaching a total population of almost 10 billion in 2050 and, in most regions, the lowest per capita income across the three scenarios. The assumed high intensity in agricultural production leads to comparatively strong exogenous growth in crop and grassland yields: based on moderate GDP growth, rapid developments of fossil energy-based technologies and moderate yield damage from climate change, yields develop relatively favourably. Energy price assumptions are extended from the IEA's Current Policy Scenario, generally assuming increasing real prices - for instance, the real price for crude oil is assumed to increase by 112% between 2010 and 2050 while that of coal would rise by only 22% over the same period. Food consumption patterns are driven mainly by population and income growth which, given these drivers, implies strong growth of demand for staples – driven by population growth – but relatively moderate growth in high-value products, which is driven largely by per capita income growth. No specific changes in trade policies are assumed. However, trade costs for food and agriculture trade between the three large world regions, including: i) the Americas, ii) Europe, the Middle East and Africa, and iii) Asia and Oceania, are assumed to increase by 10% of the traded value, given the lack of regulatory coherence resulting from the regions' focus on sovereignty and independence.

In comparison, the **Citizen-Driven, Sustainable Growth** scenario is driven by significantly lower population growth, reaching a total population of about 8.5 billion in 2050. Per capita income growth is slightly lower than in the Individual, Fossil Fuel-Driven Growth scenario for the OECD average, but higher in emerging and developing economies. Reduced input use results in yield growth well below that assumed for the Individual, Fossil Fuel-Driven Growth scenario, notably in the longer run: relatively low GDP growth within the OECD area and a move away from input-based technologies depresses average yields, despite the comparatively low impact of climate change. Energy price assumptions are higher than those in the Individual, Fossil Fuel-Driven Growth scenario, particularly in the medium-term, while the differences become smaller in the long run – the total increase in real crude oil prices is assumed to be 120%, for example, three-quarters of which occur by 2030. A major difference is assumed for food consumption patterns, resulting in significantly lower demand for livestock products, particularly meat, compared to what per capita incomes would suggest, while demand for fruits and vegetables and other nutritionally valuable food is assumed to increase well above trends, as a result of income growth. As can be seen from the model results, this demand shift is large compared to the dampened yield growth, causing somewhat lower prices overall. Trade costs related to regulatory differences are assumed to remain unchanged, i.e. no additional costs are modelled in this scenario.

Finally, the **Fast, Globally-Driven Growth** scenario is characterised by medium population growth, reaching a total population of about 9.3 billion in 2050, and strong per capita income growth in all regions. Exogenous yield assumptions are between the two other scenarios: with strong innovation and rapid spread of technologies partly offset by strong yield damage from climate change, yield growth would significantly exceed those in the Citizen-Driven, Sustainable Growth scenario while falling short of the input-intensive Individual, Fossil Fuel-Driven Growth. Assumptions for energy prices show convergence across fuel types and regions: while prices for crude oil are assumed to increase by just 41% in real terms, those for coal, which is much cheaper, are assumed to rise by 145%. Similarly, prices for natural gas in North America are assumed to rise more quickly than those in Europe and the Pacific area. Similar to the Individual, Fossil Fuel-Driven Growth scenario, food demand patterns are driven by population and income growth. In comparison, however, the Fast, Globally-Driven Growth scenario features a stronger move towards livestock and other high-value products and less towards staple crops. As a result of increased international co-operation, trade costs related to regulatory differences are assumed to decrease by 10% of the traded value for food and agriculture both within and between the large world regions.

Global production of cereals and meat has experienced significant growth over the past four decades, and this development is expected to continue towards 2050 with some modifications: most importantly, the increase in world meat production could slow significantly in the *Sustainable* scenario, given the strong move away from animal protein in consumers' diets in wealthier societies. In contrast, cereal production growth may accelerate over the coming two decades in the *Individual* and *Fast* scenarios, thanks to large productivity gains and strong population growth. On average across different models, cereal and meat production could increase by some 60% and 70% by 2050 in the *Fast* scenario and slightly less in the *Individual* scenario (Figure 1.1).

These averages however mask significant differences between the four contributing models. The variability across models, shown by the dotted lines in Figure 1.1, is of a similar magnitude to the variability across scenarios at this global level. In most cases, the main conclusions drawn from the total of the four models are fairly robust across these models. For instance, rankings between scenarios obtained from the average results across models are broadly in line with those suggested by all or most individual models. The exceptions are generally related to outcomes which are similar for different scenarios: in such cases, individual models may suggest different rankings – however, these

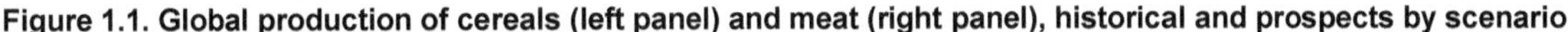

differences are then less significant. The variability across models results from different theories underpinning these. Acknowledging this variability in model outcomes is an important part of recognising, and dealing with, uncertainties.

Figure 1.1. Global production of cereals (left panel) and meat (right panel), historical and prospects by scenario

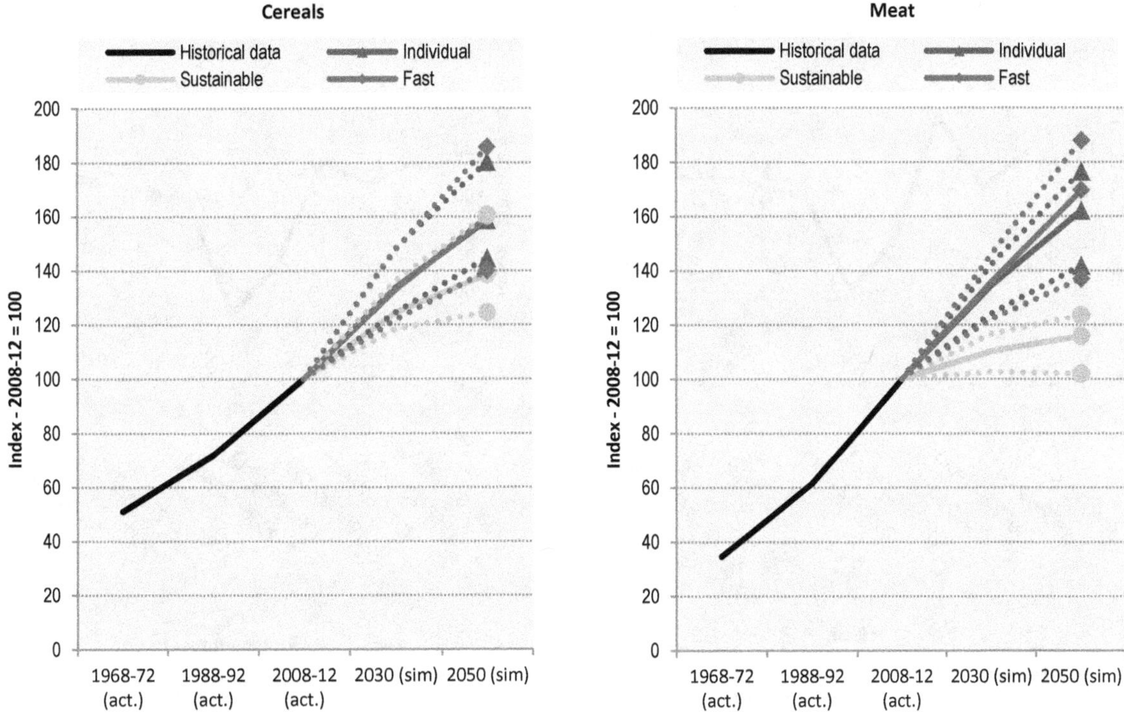

Note: Historical data is based on physical quantities, while prospects are based on production volumes valued in constant prices. Model results are relative changes in time between 2010, 2030 and 2050, superimposed on actual data from other sources, therefore prospects in levels are derived from additional calculations. Thick lines represent means across four contributing models, while dotted lines represent the range of model results (minima and maxima).

Source: Historical data from FAOSTAT (2014); prospects from results provided by contributing models. http://faostat3.fao.org/home/E.

While model results for agricultural production suggest a continuation of historical trends with some modifications, the picture looks very different for agricultural prices. Agricultural prices in real terms have fallen by almost 2% per year on average in the four decades between 1960 and 2000, but have increased significantly in the 2000s. According to the results for the three scenarios, the historical trend of falling prices is unlikely to re-emerge in the future decades. On average across models, prices for crops and other agricultural products appear unlikely to decline, but rather to remain largely flat or, in the case of the *Fast* scenario in particular – with its strong global economic growth - to increase towards 2050 (Figure 1.2). In the *Sustainable* scenario, with the shift away from livestock products in consumers' diets and the consequential reduced pressure on agricultural resources, prices for cereals are found to fall slightly, while meat and notably ruminant meat prices would continue to decline.

Where production volumes are concerned, the variability across models is large. Model results show significant differences in the *Fast* scenario in particular, with its high economic growth and strong climate change. While three of the models show changes of agricultural prices in the range between -17% and +19% over the 40-year period, the fourth model shows significantly stronger price growth in all three scenarios, with up to +60% in the *Fast* scenario.

Figure 1.2. Global real producer prices for agricultural products, historical and prospects by scenario

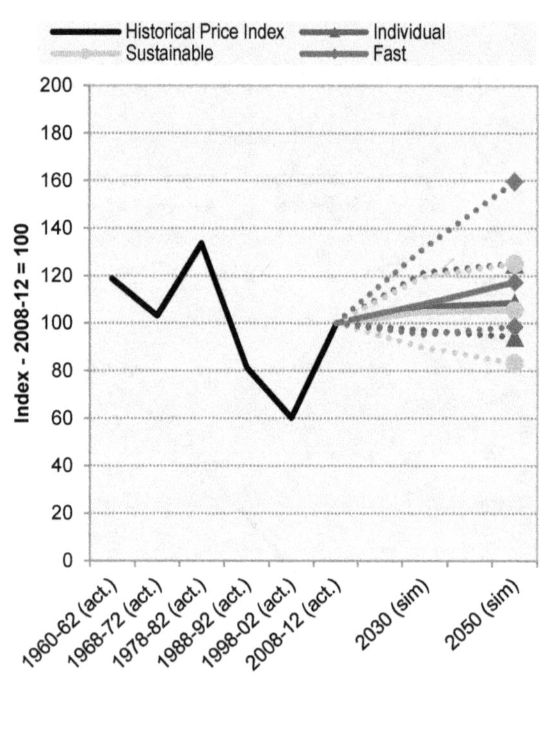

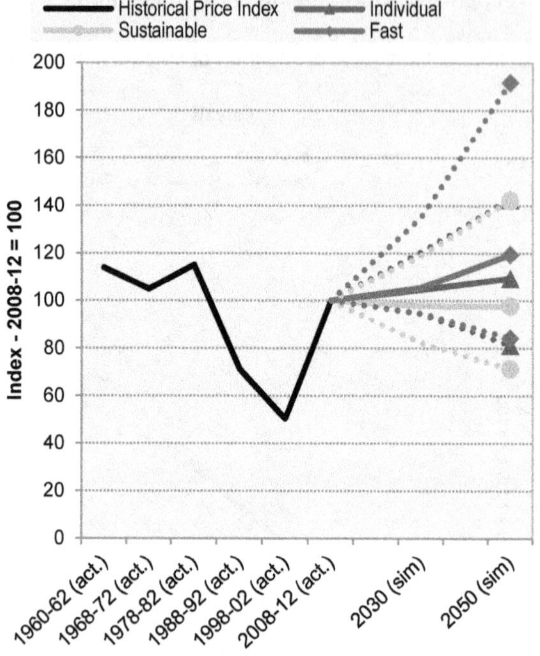

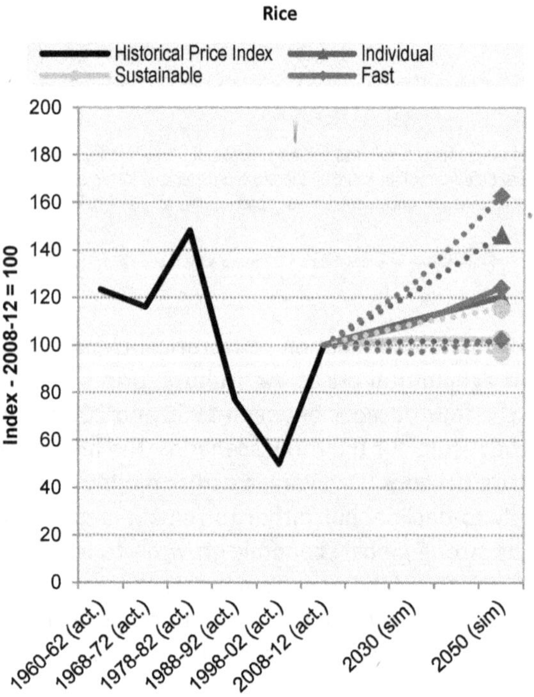

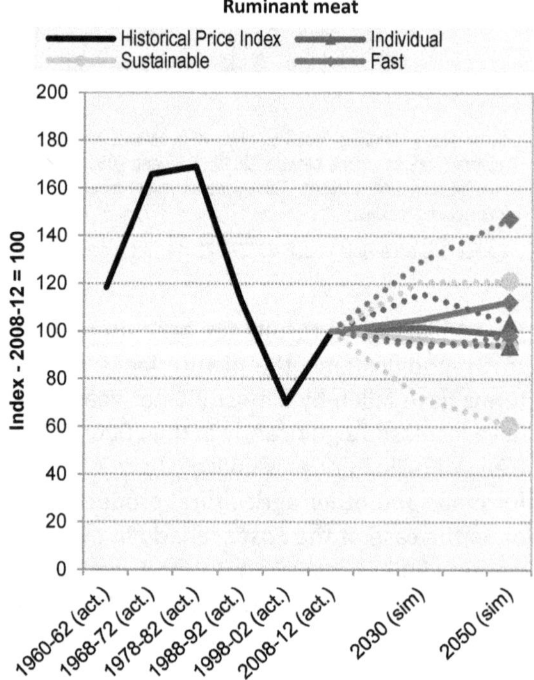

Note: Historical real commodity prices, prospects for average global real producer prices. All prices deflated based on the US GDP deflator. Model results are relative changes in time between 2010, 2030 and 2050, superimposed on actual data from other sources, therefore prospects in levels are derived from additional calculations. Thick lines represent means across four contributing models, while dotted lines represent the range of model results (minima and maxima). Historical coarse grain prices are for maize, historical rice prices are for Thai 5% broken, historical ruminant meat prices are for beef.

Sources: Historical data from World Bank (2015a), US GDP deflator from World Bank (2015b), prospects from results provided by contributing models.

Four main uncertainties are behind much of the differences in the model results: i) the development of food demand as incomes continue to grow; ii) the technical possibility and costs of bringing additional land into agricultural use; iii) the role and modelling of labour productivity in the context of growing economies; and iv) prospects for productivity responses as agricultural prices increase.[4]

In addition, given their deterministic nature, none of the models provide insights into potential developments in price volatility which may have significant implications for shorter-term developments in food security, farm economics and other variables. Shocks and volatility continue to characterise all three scenarios, although the type of shocks and the regional distribution of market swings differ. With more open economies and trade able to buffer some of the regional shocks, the volatility of markets is likely to be of a more global and often dampened nature in the *Fast* scenario, whereas the *Individual* scenario is characterised by political and climate instability of a regional focus, with less buffering from international markets. The low use of farm inputs in the *Sustainable* scenario may result in higher yield fluctuations, again potentially aggravating regional market volatility.

Continuing historical trends, and notwithstanding flat or possibly higher price levels, the agricultural share in GDP is found to decrease across all regions, scenarios and models. While globally, this share has fallen from 6.4% in 1995 to around 3% today (World Bank, 2015b), model results suggest that it would reach levels between 1.6% (*Individual*) and 1.2% (*Fast* scenario) by 2050.[5] While the importance of agriculture within the overall economy is much larger in developing countries, the declining trend – a result of overall growth – is found across the board and is mirrored and emphasised by shrinking shares in total labour use.

Notes

1. While a number of "developing countries" are likely to change status and become more developed over time, this and similar terms are used throughout this report to distinguish country groups based on their current economic status.

2. The Convention on Biological Diversity defines biodiversity as "the variability among living organisms from all sources including, inter alia, terrestrial, marine and other aquatic ecosystems and the ecological complexes of which they are part; this includes diversity within species, between species and of ecosystems" (Article 2, CBD, 1992).

3. More recent research based on satellite imagery suggests that this commonly accepted assertion of deceleration may not be true, however. According to a paper accepted by Geophysical Research Letters, net losses of forest cover in the humid tropics – tropical Africa, Southeast Asia and Latin America – have increased from an average of 4 million ha per year during the 1990s to an average 6.5 million ha per year during the 2000s. The authors do however find a smaller decrease from the first to the second quintennium of the 2000s, from 7 million ha per year between 2000 and 2005 to 6.1 million ha per year between 2005 and 2010, due to greater forest gains in tropical Asia and slowing losses in Brazil (Kim et al., 2015).

4. This holds true for a larger number of models that are used for long term projections. See von Lampe et al. (2014a), Robinson et al. (2014) and several other papers within the same special issue of *Agricultural Economics* (Vol. 45/1).

5. Using World Bank estimates for 2008-12 and growth rates from model results.

References

Alexandratos, N. and J. Bruinsma (2012), *World Agriculture Towards 2030/2050: The 2012 Revision,* ESA Working Paper, No. 12/03, Food and Agriculture Organization, Rome, www.fao.org/fileadmin/templates/esa/Global_persepctives/world_ag_2030_50_2012_rev.pdf.

AMIS (2015), *Market Monitor 25 – February 2015*, Agricultural Market Information System, www.amis-outlook.org/amis-monitoring (accessed 29 October 2015).

CBD (1992), *Convention on Biological Diversity*, United Nations, www.cbd.int/convention/text/default.shtml.

Comprehensive Assessment of Water Management in Agriculture (2007), *Water for Food, Water for Life: A Comprehensive Assessment of Water Management in Agriculture*, Earthscan and International Water Management Institute, London and Colombo, www.fao.org/nr/water/docs/summary_synthesisbook.pdf.

Cordell, D., J.-O. Drangert and S. White (2009), "The story of phosphorus: Global food security and food for thought", *Traditional Peoples and Climate Change,* Vol. 19/2, pp. 292-305, Elsevier, www.sciencedirect.com/science/article/pii/S095937800800099X.

Dorin, B., S. Treyer and S. Paillard, eds. (2011), *Scenarios and Challenges for Feeding the World in 2050,* INRA and CIRAD, Paris, summary (from 2009) available at www.paris.inra.fr/depe/Media/Fichier/Prospectives/Agrimonde/Synthese-du-rapport, or www.cirad.fr/en/content/download/3796/35063/version/7/file/1209Agrimonde_SummaryReport.pdf.

Elsner, H. (2008), "Stand der Phosphat-Reserven Weltweit", presentation given at the "Braunschweiger Nährstofftage 2008", Germany, www.pcs-consult.de/Phosphat-Reserven.pdf.

Eswaran, H., R. Lal and P.F. Reich (2001), "Land degradation: An overview" in Bridges, E.M. et al. (eds.), *Responses to Land Degradation*, Proc. 2nd. International Conference on Land Degradation and Desertification, Khon Kaen, Thailand. Oxford Press, New Delhi, India, www.nrcs.usda.gov/wps/portal/nrcs/detail/soils/use/?cid=nrcs142p2_054028.

FAO (2014a), *The State of Food Insecurity in the World 2014*, Food and Agriculture Organization, Rome, http://www.fao.org/3/a-i4030e.pdf.

FAO (2014b), *Food Outlook October 2014*, Food and Agriculture Organization, Rome, www.fao.org/Giews/english/fo/index.htm (accessed 29 October 2015).

FAOSTAT (2014), Statistical Data of the Food and Agriculture Organization website, Food and Agriculture Organization, Rome, http://faostat3.fao.org/home/E (accessed 28 November 2014).

Foresight (2011), *The Future of Food and Farming: Challenges and Choices for Global Sustainability*, Final Project Report, The Government Office for Science, London, www.gov.uk/government/publications/future-of-food-and-farming.

GLASOD (1990), Global Assessment of Human-induced Soil Degradation (GLASOD) website, www.isric.org/projects/global-assessment-human-induced-soil-degradation-glasod (accessed 29 October 2015).

Grantham, J. (2011) "Time to wake up: Days of abundant resources and falling prices are over forever", *GMO Quarterly Letter,* April 2011, CFA Institute, www.cfainstitute.org (accessed 29 October 2015).

IEA (2014), *World Energy Outlook 2014*, IEA, Paris, http://dx.doi.org/10.1787/weo-2014-en.

IPCC (2014), *Climate Change 2014: Impacts, Adaptation, and Vulnerability. Working Group II Contribution to the Fifth Assessment Report of the Intergovernmental Panel on Climate Change*, Cambridge University Press, Cambridge and New York, www.ipcc-wg2.gov/AR5.

IPCC (2013), *Climate Change 2013: The Physical Basis. Working Group I Contribution to the Fifth Assessment Report of the Intergovernmental Panel on Climate Change*, Cambridge University Press, Cambridge and New York, www.ipcc.ch/report/ar5.

IPCC (2000), *Emissions Scenarios*, International Governmental Panel on Climate Change, Cambridge University Press, United Kingdom, www.ipcc.ch/ipccreports/sres/emission/index.php?idp=0.

Kali and Salz (undated), "Global potash deposits", www.k-plus-s.com/en/wissen/rohstoffe/index.html (accessed 29 October 2015).

Kim, D.-H., J.O. Sexton and J.R. Townshend (2015), "Accelerated deforestation in the humid tropics from the 1990s to the 2000s", paper accepted for publication in *Geophysical Research Letters*, Vol. 42/9, http://onlinelibrary.wiley.com/doi/10.1002/2014GL062777/abstract.

Mineweb (2013), "The huge potential of Congo potash", www.mineweb.com/archive/the-huge-potential-of-congo-potash.

Nelson, G.C. et al. (2010), *Food Security, Farming, and Climate Change to 2050: Scenarios, Results, Policy Options*, International Food Policy Research Institute, Washington, D.C. www.ifpri.org/publication/food-security-farming-and-climate-change-2050.

OECD/FAO (2014a), *OECD-FAO Agricultural Outlook 2014*, OECD Publishing, Paris, http://dx.doi.org/10.1787/agr_outlook-2014-en

OECD (2014b), *OECD Economic Outlook,* Issue 2/96, November 2014, OECD Publishing Paris, http://dx.doi.org/10.1787/eco_outlook-v2014-2-en.

OECD (2013a), "Overweight and obesity", *OECD Factbook 2013: Economic, Environmental and Social Statistics*, OECD Publishing, Paris, http://dx.doi.org/10.1787/factbook-2013-100-en.

OECD (2012), *OECD Environmental Outlook to 2050: The Consequences of Inaction*, OECD Publishing, Paris, http://dx.doi.org/10.1787/9789264122246-en.

Robinson, S. et al. (2014), "Comparing supply-side specifications in models of global agriculture and the food system", *Agricultural Economics*, Vol. 45/1, pp. 21-35, http://onlinelibrary.wiley.com/doi/10.1111/agec.12087/abstract.

Slingenberg, A. et al. (2009), *Study on Understanding the Causes of Biodiversity Loss and the Policy Assessment Framework: Final Report*, European Commission, Directorate-General for Environment, Brussels, http://ec.europa.eu/environment/enveco/biodiversity/pdf/causes_biodiv_loss.pdf.

United Nations (2005), *United Nations Millennium Ecosystem Assessment*, www.millenniumassessment.org/en/About.html#1 (accessed 29 October 2015).

UNEP (2012), *GEO 5 Global Environment Outlook: Environment for the Future We Want*, United Nations Environment Programme, Valletta, www.unep.org/geo/pdfs/geo5/GEO5_report_full_en.pdf.

UNEP (2009), *International Assessment of Agricultural Knowledge, Science and Technology for Development*, www.unep.org/dewa/Assessments/Ecosystems/IAASTD/tabid/105853/Default.aspx (accessed 29 October 2015).

Van Dijk, M. and G.W. Meijerink (2014), "A review of global food security scenario and assessment studies: results, gaps and research priorities", *Global Food Security* 3(2014), pp. 227-238, www.sciencedirect.com/science/article/pii/S2211912414000388

Von Lampe, M. et al. (2014), "Why do global long-term scenarios for agriculture differ? An overview of the AgMIP Global Economic Model Intercomparison", *Agricultural Economics*, Vol. 45/1, pp. 3-20, http://onlinelibrary.wiley.com/doi/10.1111/agec.12086/abstract.

WHO (2015): *Global Health Observatory Data Repository* (database), http://apps.who.int/gho/data/?theme=main (accessed 29 October 2015).

World Bank (2015a), *Pink Data. Historical price series* (database), http://go.worldbank.org/4ROCCIEQ50 (accessed February 2015).

World Bank (2015b), *World Development Indicators* (database), http://data.worldbank.org/data-catalog/world-development-indicators (accessed February 2015).

Annex 1.A1

Storylines and drivers within the three alternate scenarios

Individual, Fossil Fuel-Driven Growth

In the Individual, Fossil Fuel-Driven Growth world, a world where national and regional focus on independence and growth dominates, little emphasis is given to environmental or social questions beyond short-term responses to emerging problems.

Storyline

In the wake of unsuccessful negotiations on a global trade agreement, and the failure of climate talks, governments increasingly turn their attention to domestic interests and those of their immediate neighbours. Global governance is less and less relied upon. Instead, regional agreements and other forms of regional co-operation are based on specific national interests, such as the development of markets for resource-rich countries towards large populous neighbours. These regional agreements tend to be large enough to ensure sufficiently big markets, although the depth of co-operation remains rather limited and is based on immediate gains rather than longer-term trust-building and regulatory coherence. Global value chains are increasingly complemented – and to some degree replaced by – regional value chains, taking advantage of the development of regional trade agreements.

Technological and method developments focus on the efficient extraction of fossil energy sources where these are available. For instance, the exploitation of shale gas and shale oil, which is increasing in North America, expands to include the Russian Federation, the People's Republic of China, South America and Europe.[1] Commercial exploitation of methane from large methane hydrate reserves begins in northern Russia and the northern part of the Chinese Sea. Other large sources of energy include coal conversion and off-shore oil. Bioenergy is seen as a solution for energy resource-constrained but relatively land-abundant regions.

Certain regions, such as the Middle East and parts of Africa, continue to be vulnerable to political instability. As a consequence, economic and societal developments remain slower in these regions than elsewhere, given lower investments, weaker trade integration, lack of infrastructure etc. In other parts of the world, industrialised regions in particular, technological developments, intense exploitation of fossil energy sources, and reasonable growth in trade within the regional blocks all combine to create significant income growth. However, with limited international co-operation, continued political instability in some regions and a strong focus on fossil energy, inequalities both across and within countries increase. Growth in many developing countries remains much more limited than their potential would suggest, and is below the OECD average.

1. The US Energy Information Administration estimates global technically recoverable resources of shale oil and shale gas to be more than four times those in North America alone (www.eia.gov/analysis/studies/worldshalegas).

Within the majority of countries, the influence of civil society organisations remains rather limited. Instead, central governments hold the most power, playing a key role in defending the interests of national populations.

Early signs

"Methane hydrates could be the energy of the future" (*Financial Times*, 17 January 2014).

"The conference which was supposed to find a replacement for Kyoto – Copenhagen in 2009 – was a comprehensive failure. There is at present no reason to suppose that the next major international conference on which hopes now rest – Paris in 2015 – will succeed." (*The Guardian*, 22 July 2013).

Implications for key drivers

Population growth remains strong in both developed and developing countries. Global population reaches close to 10 billion by 2050, with little deceleration over time. Population growth continues virtually unchecked in many developing countries: while between 2010 and 2050, populations in the OECD area and the BRIICS countries (Brazil, Russian Federation, India, Indonesia, China and South Africa) grow by 25% and 18%, respectively, the population of the rest of the world grows by 84% over the same period. This population growth comes with increased urbanisation, a development that is most evident in Africa and developing Asia. Urban centres remain key food consumers but continue to contribute very little to food production.

Per capita incomes increase across all regions, although existing inequalities become more pronounced both across and within countries and regions. Global per capita GDP more than doubles between 2010 and 2050, corresponding to a 2% per year growth per capita, or 2.9% per year total growth. Developing countries outside the BRIICS barely grow faster, on a per capita basis, than OECD countries, with a number growing much more slowly. Income distribution within countries becomes more unequal in all regions, particularly in today's emerging economies, China, India and Indonesia.

Energy markets remain relatively segregated across fossil sources and, for gas, across regions. Crude oil prices roughly double in real terms between 2010 and 2050, as do prices for natural gas in most regions. Coal prices, in contrast, increase by just 22% thanks to abundant exploitation and little environmental regulation, and fuel significant shares of energy consumption in China and other Asian countries.

Productivity growth in agriculture is high, driven by significant investments in R&D from both public and private sources. This, together with intensive use of farm inputs, offsets some of the negative impacts from increasingly scarce natural resources, including water. Average crop yields therefore continue to grow rapidly.

As a result of societies' limited interest in sustainable development, patterns of food consumption are characterised by the high intake of animal products and other high-value products where consumers can afford them. Even in richer countries, little emphasis is given to environmental, societal or quality attributes, which therefore do not represent relevant characteristics of the food supply.

Due to the focus on fossil energy use and the lack of environmental consciousness in consumer choices, GHG emissions continue to rise significantly, dampened only by the moderate growth of many economies. This in turn has negative consequences for the climate.

Citizen-Driven, Sustainable Growth

In a world driven by civil societies' focus on environmental and social wellbeing, individual countries take regional leads in greening their economies, while little progress is made towards finding global solutions.

Storyline

A combination of increasing concerns about natural resources and environmental damages, and growing mistrust in international institutions, leads ever-growing segments of populations to engage in grass-roots initiatives which look for alternative pathways. While this movement first develops in Western Europe in particular, it quickly expands to other industrialised countries, followed by emerging and, eventually, developing economies. A variety of bottom-up approaches develops, all driven by consumers and citizens with a strong focus on sustainable development and consumption patterns. Increasingly, civil society organisations also include social aspects within their portfolios of interest and activity. The environmental and social footprint of food and other products is considered to be an important factor in many everyday decisions, not only decisions on food consumption. People engage in the sustainable development of transportation systems, the planning of agglomerations and many other areas.

In contrast, global co-operation is much less of a concern to people, and the funding of international institutions and organisations becomes increasingly difficult. Individual countries develop different strategies for greening their economies. Neighbouring countries with similar conditions adopt the strategies of leader countries. Co-operation is therefore largely limited to exchange and harmonise systems within regions. National governments are carefully monitored and strongly influenced by civil society organisations and hence tend to act less independently than in 2015.

Most research and development efforts are focused on natural resource savings and environment preservation. Although methods and technologies spill over relatively easily within regions, transfer between regions is lacking.

Within countries and regions, enhanced social engagement improves access to resources such as food, wealth, education and technologies for all segments of society. Better education results in lower fertility and better health status, which in turn improve productivity in various industries and sectors, agriculture included.

Consistent with the more regional focus of co-operation, and responding to consumer demand for more local and regional food sourcing where possible, there is a shift away from global towards regional value chains. Where regional coalitions are sufficiently large, this does not reduce the efficiency of these chains, although there is an increased risk of disruptions due to changing regional agreements.

Early signs

"Organic UK food sales defy market downturn to rise 4% in 2014" (*The Guardian*, 24 February 2015).

"Rebound in clean energy investment in 2014 beats expectations. Surges in investment in offshore wind in Europe, and solar in China and the United States, helped to drive the 2014 global clean energy total up 16% to USD 310bn" (*Bloomberg New Energy Finance*, 9 January 2015).

Implications for key drivers

Population growth significantly slows down relative to current trends. Global population remains under 8.5 billion by 2050, with little growth remaining towards the end of this period. The population of the BRIICS countries peaks around 2040, driven by falling population numbers in China since the early 2020s. The total OECD population grows by about a fifth. Even in developing countries, population growth is showing a marked slow-down – average population growth in the rest of the world declines to half a percent per year between 2040 and 2050. In parallel, the trend towards mega-cities also decelerates, as citizens' interest in living in, or close to, green environments drives movement from large agglomerations to smaller cities and towns in many industrialised countries. This movement stimulates increased urban agriculture, which supplies consumers with fresh local produce such as vegetables and fruits.

A better education system and significant R&D efforts in the efficient use of natural resources strongly improves productivities in many sectors. As a consequence, per capita incomes rise strongly, and existing inequalities both across and within countries decline. Helped also by lower population growth, global per capita GDP increases by 177% between 2010 and 2050, corresponding to a 2.6% per year growth per capita. Growth is most pronounced in emerging and developing countries, while the increase of per capita incomes within the OECD remains relatively low, at 1.6% per year over the four decades, contributing to a narrowing income gap between OECD and other countries.

Energy markets show signs of scarcity in the short- to medium-term, as investments in fossil sources slow down. It is only in the longer-run that investments in new technologies – both in alternative energy sources and in energy-saving appliances and methods – result in demand effects which are sufficient to slow energy price rises. Crude oil prices increase by 120% between 2010 and 2050, with three-quarters of this increase occurring by 2030. Natural gas prices show a similar development, with strong price increases by 2030, followed by flatter price paths thereafter. Demand for coal declines first in OECD countries, while large supplies in Asia enable prices to remain fairly stable.

Given high investments in R&D, largely from public sources, productivity growth in agriculture is quite high and focuses on the efficient use of natural resources. Due to the more restricted use of farm inputs, however, growth in average crop yields is comparatively low, notably in the longer-run.

As a result of strong public interest in sustainable and healthy diets, food consumption patterns are characterised by the limited intake of red meat and other animal products, and greater shares of vegetable products. Environmental, societal and quality attributes represent important characteristics of the food supply.

As a consequence of the reduced focus on fossil energy use, lower input use in agriculture and the increasing importance of the carbon footprint as a variable in consumer choices, GHG emissions peak in 2020 and fall strongly towards 2050. Negative consequences for the climate therefore remain rather limited.

Fast, Globally-Driven Growth

In the Fast, Globally-Driven Growth world, governments are strongly focused on economic growth and international co-operation on economic, social and political issues. Environmental issues receive less attention.

Storyline

Following the final adoption of the "Bali Package", the world witnesses a revival of multilateral institutions and negotiations, notably with the Agreement on Trade Facilitation in November 2014. In 2015, the 21st Session of the Conference of the Parties to the UNFCCC in Paris secures a strong commitment to increase the carbon efficiencies of economic growth, even if this is insufficient to prevent further increasing emissions as economies continue to grow. In 2019, a strong focus on multilateral co-operation in international trade bears fruit in the form of a far-reaching global trade agreement, facilitated by the WTO. One year later, the food multinationals Nestlé and Unilever, the retail giants Tesco and Carrefour, online market place Ebay, the seed powerhouses DuPont and Syngenta, and several agro-tech companies all sign a comprehensive agreement on joint research and development work to enhance productivity along the entire food supply chain.

Backed by strong international co-operation and driven by the major engines of growth – China, India, Brazil and some South Asian economies – innovation and trade foster global economic development. The rush into new technologies and production methods for food, feed and energy helps to meet the needs of a significantly expanding global population while coping with looming resource scarcities. In addition to the efficient exploitation and use of fossil fuels, alternative energy technologies including hydrogen and fuel cells, electric vehicles, biomass-based fuels and chemistry help to satisfy energy demands, and remote sensing and the omnipresent internet of things improves production processes including in agriculture.

In this strongly market-driven system, global economic growth accelerates to more than 4% towards 2030, with only little slowdown thereafter. Food consumption patterns become increasingly similar across regions, and food and cultural diversity diminishes in favour of efficiency. With rapid urbanisation and the sprawling of mega-cities in virtually all parts of the world, biodiversity becomes much less of a focus.

Most important decisions are taken either by the boards of large multinational companies or by the mayors of large cities, who gain significant power and influence. In contrast, national governments, which have sacrificed a degree of national sovereignty within multilateral agreements, see their influence decline. This also affects international organisations which have little direct links to the industry.

The rapid growth is accompanied by growing international trade in goods and services and strong increases in food production. Not everyone wins, however, and discrepancies are significant. Income and wealth inequalities rise both between and within countries. In spite of consistent economic growth in Sub-Saharan Africa, access to basic resources such as food, water and education remains difficult for a significant part of the population. Shortages in certain commodities or raw materials, due to transitions in consumption patterns, crop failures or limited reserves, repeatedly disrupt international supply chains. Europe, the Americas and the Black Sea region maintain their position as the backbone of stable agricultural production, and markets provide some form of a safety net for the rest of the world.

Early signs

"India strikes deal with US over food, breathing new life into Doha trade talks" (*The Guardian*, 13 November 2014).

"I am more confident we can achieve a global climate change deal than I have ever been before." (Ed Davey, UK Energy Secretary; quoted by the *Financial Times*, 14 December 2014).

Implications for key drivers

Global population increases by more than one-third between 2010 and 2050, reaching 9.3 billion and still growing considerably. The population of the OECD area increases by more than a fifth, partly as a result of increased migration. The BRIICS countries' population meanwhile grows by 16% by 2050, while that of the rest of the world increases by two-thirds. All of the population growth occurs within urban areas, with vast mega-cities sprawling far out from their centres. Given sophisticated infrastructure systems, including well-developed urban transportation, these urban centres function relatively well.

With substantial technological innovation and the significant use of resource-intensive inputs, incomes grow rapidly. Per capita incomes increase by an average of 3% globally between 2010 and 2050, with some developing countries quickly catching up. Average incomes in the BRIICS countries, which previously stood at 9% of the OECD average, reach 32% by 2050. Nevertheless, income disparities *within* countries in particular remain high, as the system favours capital incomes over wages.

Energy markets change significantly. Thanks to enhanced possibilities to convert both solid and gaseous fuels into liquids and vice versa, there is strong price convergence between different energy carriers, raising the price of coal relative to other fuels. Greater international trade flows result in better integration of North American shale gas with international energy markets, thus raising prices on the American market. At the same time, large-scale exploitation of new energy sources, such as methane, dampen the overall price push. As a consequence, crude oil prices increase by just 41% between 2010 and 2050, while coal and North American natural gas prices rise by 145% over the same period.

Driven by international co-operation in R&D, which is mainly funded by the private sector, agriculture exhibits fairly strong productivity growth and, together with the strong use of agricultural inputs, agricultural yields continue to rise steadily, notwithstanding the dampening effects of strong climate change and limitations in natural resources, notably water.

Strong income growth in most regions of the world drive food consumption patterns towards the high intake of animal products and other high-value products. Although wealthier consumers increasingly move towards high-quality products, there is relatively little focus on environmental or societal attributes within the overall food supply.

Notwithstanding a strong push for energy efficiency, the rapidly growing economies continue to increase their total GHG emissions well beyond current levels. As a consequence, global GHG emissions continue to rise significantly, and climate change leads to significant changes in regional temperature and precipitation patterns. The outcomes include not only frequent crop failures, but also increased risks of floods and storms.

Chapter 2

Overview of main challenges and opportunities in food and agriculture

A large number of challenges to the future of agriculture have been identified within the OECD work on Long-Term Scenarios for Food and Agriculture. This chapter explores the following seven challenges in further depth within the context of the three long-term scenarios: i) food and nutrition security, ii) economic sustainability of farming; iii) biodiversity and scarcity of natural resources; iv) agricultural greenhouse gas emissions and other pollution; v) diets and nutrition; vi) trans-boundary livestock diseases and vii) food safety. While the three "worlds" of Individual, Fossil Fuel-Driven Growth, of Citizen-Driven, Sustainable Growth and of Fast, Globally-Driven Growth all present common risks, such as those related to the environment, their magnitude varies substantially between scenarios. The performance of each of these scenarios is compared in order to facilitate the identification of strategies to manage risks and avail of future opportunities, which will be discussed in Chapter 3.

Food and nutrition security, the health of ecosystems and climate change are key elements of the ongoing debate regarding the future ability of the agricultural system to provide mankind with the products and services which it requires. A large number of challenges have been identified within the OECD work on Long-Term Scenarios for Food and Agriculture.[1] Seven broad topics, listed below, were chosen for a more detailed analysis within the context of these scenarios, of which the first five allowed for some quantification with the help of the economic models, at least to some degree:

- Food and nutrition security
- Economic sustainability of farming
- Biodiversity and scarcity of natural resources
- Agricultural greenhouse gas emissions and other pollution
- Diets and nutrition
- Trans-boundary livestock diseases
- Food safety.

Improving food and nutrition security

Food and nutrition security covers a wide range of conditions that need to be met for the nutritional wellbeing of individuals, households, and populations. Generally, food and nutrition security is defined around four pillars or dimensions, including the availability, stability, access and utilisation by the body: "Food security exists when all people, at all times, have physical, social and economic access to sufficient, safe and nutritious food to meet their dietary needs and food preferences for an active and healthy life" (FAO, 1996, 2009). The economic models used in this analysis provide a more limited view on food and nutrition security. All models generate data on production and prices of foodstuffs, but only the two partial equilibrium models calculate estimates for the per capita calorie availability, an important indicator for the availability of food at the national and regional level. In addition, the IMPACT model provides estimates for the number of malnourished children.

As noted above, the world has made significant progress towards improved food security over the past two decades. This is partly related to significantly higher food availability at both the global and regional level, a trend that is projected to continue between 2010 and 2050 (Figure 3). Moreover, while the times of significantly falling real agricultural prices may be over, this does not necessarily imply a dramatic deterioration in future global food security. Instead, some of the drivers behind improved food security, including economic growth and the development of larger middle-classes in emerging and developing economies in particular, could contribute to lifting prices above their long-term historical trend.

Nevertheless, the progress varies substantially across the three scenarios. Gains in per capita food availability are most pronounced in the Fast, Globally-Driven Growth scenario (the "*Fast*" scenario in short), combining strong income growth with significant progress in agricultural productivity and open markets. Both globally and in most regions, this scenario would continue the food availability trend of recent decades. In contrast, the Individual, Fossil Fuel-Driven Growth scenario (the "*Individual*" scenario in short) is based firmly on sovereignty and regionalism and would slow down progress substantially, as evident in much lower growth in per capita food availability both at the global and regional levels. The Citizen-Driven, Sustainable Growth scenario (the "*Sustainable*" scenario) falls between the two other scenarios. The consumption of meat and other livestock products falls below levels reached in other scenarios, particularly for the most industrialised and the emerging economies, releasing important production resources and hence reducing prices for agricultural products in general when compared to other scenarios. This effect more than offsets lower yields due to higher energy costs and constraints on input use. In many developing countries therefore, total calorie availability increases to levels similar to those in the *Fast* scenario, but more importantly, the average dietary composition improves in these countries.

The consequences of higher food availability are potentially significant reductions in the prevalence of hunger – even if the regional totals mask the unequal distribution within populations and do not shed light on the effects of temporary shocks and volatility. Progress towards reduced malnutrition is likely to remain relatively limited in an *Individual* world, as income growth and the ability of international markets to compensate for regional production shortfalls are more limited than in the two other scenarios. Indeed, IMPACT simulations suggest that in the *Individual* scenario, the absolute number of malnourished children in Sub-Saharan Africa could increase towards 2030 and fall only slightly between 2030 and 2050. Globally, this indicator improves by 15% in this scenario, 36% in the *Fast* scenario, and 44% in the *Sustainable* scenario,[2] suggesting that significant progress can be made, but that the context matters significantly. A key driver behind the reduction of malnourishment is the income growth embedded within the scenarios, which in turn supports agricultural prices through higher food demand. As the IMPACT model for these two scenarios simulates relatively high prices for agricultural products when compared to the other models, progress implied by the other models' results might be even stronger.

People will benefit to different degrees from increased food availability. The greater focus on social balancing and the reduction of income inequalities should help to further reduce poverty and malnutrition for more households in the *Sustainable* scenario. In contrast, growing income disparities in the *Fast* scenario, and in the *Individual* scenario in particular, are likely to reduce the overall beneficial effects of growing food availability.

In addition, beyond this static view on food availability and food access, food and nutrition security is driven to a significant degree by the stability of agriculture and food systems. Substantial progress can be made to reduce chronic hunger in a *Fast* world in particular, due to strong income growth in developing countries, reduced international trade costs, and yield and productivity growth enhanced by global co-operation and trans-regional technological spill-overs. At the same time, however, strong climate change in both the *Individual* and *Fast* scenarios are likely to increase risks related to extreme weather events, such as droughts and floods, storms or excessive precipitation. Open trade and international engagement in information exchange may mitigate some of the negative consequences for temporary regional food shortages, adding to the benefits of the more rapid economic growth exhibited within the *Fast* scenario. Meanwhile, transitional food insecurity may add to chronic malnourishment in the *Sustainable* scenario, as the reduced use of farm inputs risks making regional agricultural output more variable, and the lesser degree of economic integration through the global trading system reduces the capacity of international markets to buffer such regional shocks.

The economic sustainability of farming

The economic sustainability of farming is of prime importance for the performance of the sector overall, and of key interest for agricultural ministries in most countries. As is the case for business in general, the economic performance of farms depends on a large number of factors, including – but not limited to – productivity growth and the development of appropriate skills within farm households and enterprises. Given much of the sector's dependence on land and other natural resources for its production, limits to the availability of these factors will also drive the economics of farming at the farm, regional and global levels.

Figure 2.1. Per capita food availability at the global level (upper left panel), in Africa and Middle East (upper right panel), South Asia (lower left panel) and South and Central America (lower right panel), 1970-2050

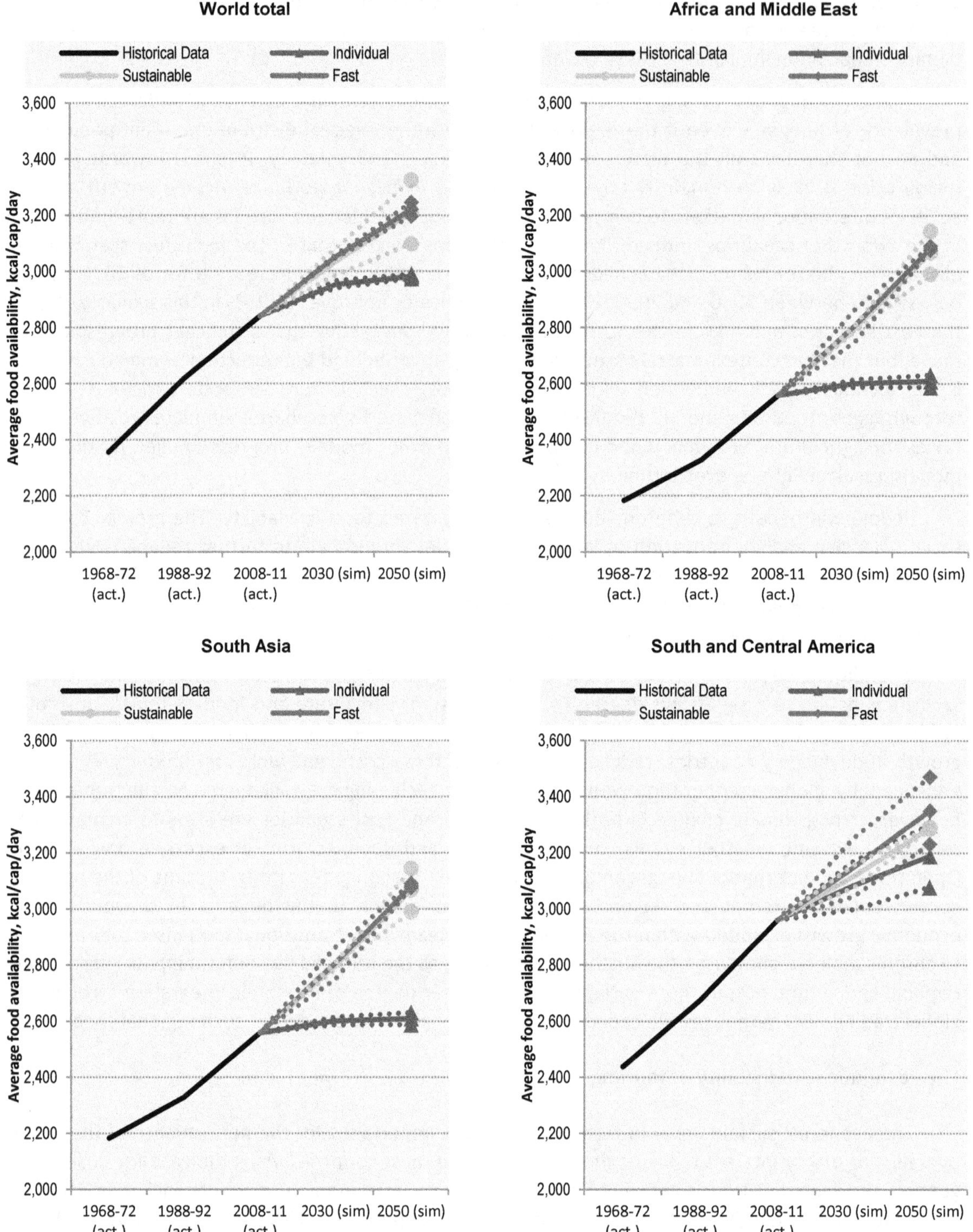

Note: Thick lines represent means across the two PE models providing calorie data, while dotted lines represent the range of model results (minima and maxima). Model results are relative changes in time between 2010, 2030 and 2050, superimposed on actual data from other sources, therefore prospects in levels are derived from additional calculations. Additional results for North America, Europe and Oceania are available in Annex C.

Source: Historical data from FAOSTAT (2014); prospects from results provided by contributing models.

With average agricultural prices stable or increasing over the coming decades, the rising output required from primary agriculture should frame profitable conditions for farming. Results from the two CGE models suggest that globally, farm incomes – i.e. value added for labour, capital and land employed in primary agriculture – should increase by between 50% and 150% in real terms (about 1.1% to 2.3% p.a. on average) between 2010 and 2050, depending on the scenario and the model. Growth appears to be more pronounced in the *Sustainable* and *Fast* scenarios, more than doubling on average across the two models, strongly driven by developments in Asia, Africa and the Middle East, whereas farm incomes would rise by less than 80% in the *Individual* world. Greater international exchange and sustainable productivity growth both contribute to better prospects for farm incomes.

Rapid growth in per capita incomes also helps to raise farm incomes, particularly in developing countries in the *Fast* and *Sustainable* scenarios. Farming in Latin America would particularly prosper, notably in a globalised world, which continues to consume a lot of meat (Figure 2.2). Less meat-rich diets, in contrast, would benefit farming in Asia and Africa, where livestock production is relatively less important. Asian farm incomes would rise by 176% in the *Sustainable* scenario, taking the average of the two models. While farm incomes in Oceania are also found to rise significantly, prospects are less favourable in North America and, notably, Europe. In the latter region, farm incomes are found to barely change in real terms. Europe would see farm incomes put under pressure by a more globalised world which would favour other sectors in this region. Here, and in contrast to other regions, only the *Individual* scenario, with its high fossil input use and less open markets, shows an increase in average farm incomes.

These averages again mask possible distributional differences. In the *Fast* scenario in particular, small and subsistence farms in developing countries, with limited access to large markets and value chains, may find it difficult to benefit from rising farm incomes as much as more integrated farms or those linked to specific consumer markets can. In addition, potentially reduced competition between a limited number of large multinational firms may make it difficult for farms to reap the full benefits of these developments if and when market power is executed. The growth in average farm incomes also needs to be put into perspective with developments within the overall economy: labour and capital incomes outside the agricultural sector are modelled to grow by 240% and 380% globally over the same period.

Structural change within the agricultural sector, including developments in the number and size of individual farm operations, is another key factor in the economic sustainability of farming.[3] Recent history suggests very different developments between developed and developing countries in this respect. While consistent and comprehensive data on farm numbers and farm sizes across time and countries are not available, the FAO's World Programme for the Census of Agriculture (FAO, 2010) provides some evidence. Between 1970 and 2000,[4] most European countries have seen the number of farms decline by up to 4% per year on average. The same holds for developed countries in North America, Asia and Oceania – although this trend has only relatively recently emerged in New Zealand. At the same time, average farm *sizes* in these countries have increased accordingly. In contrast, farm numbers in African and Asian countries have increased in recent decades, and farms have become smaller on average. Declining farm numbers in the majority of developed countries have raised concerns in governments and societies alike regarding the protection of family heritage, landscape conservation and the development of rural areas. The fragmentation of agricultural holdings in parts of the developing world, on the other hand, may accentuate poverty among resource-poor, low-productivity farmers.

Figure 2.2. Growth in real farm incomes, 2010 to 2050

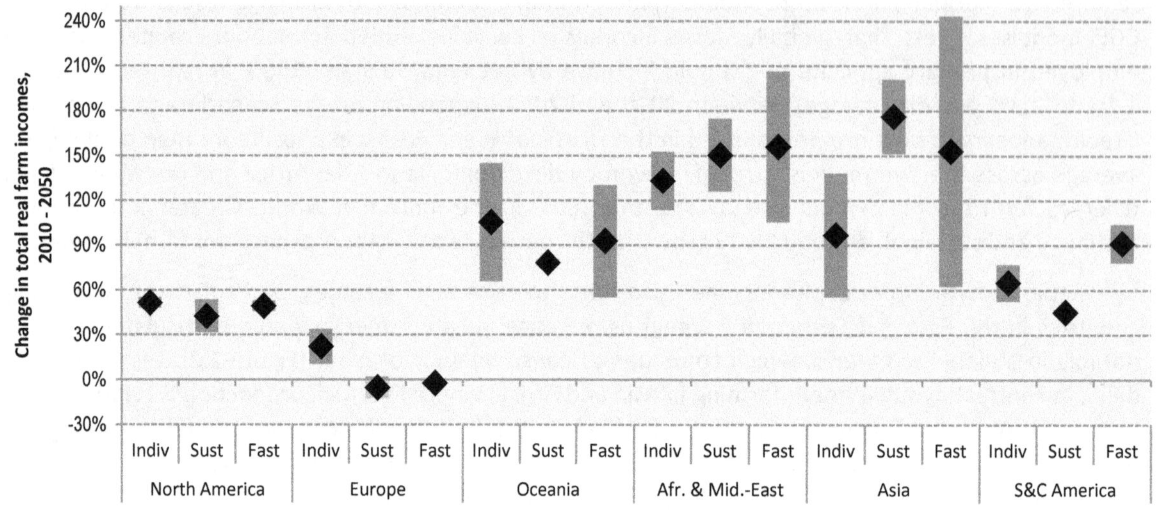

Note: Farm incomes are represented as the value added for labour, capital and land employed in primary agriculture.

Source: Results provided by the ENVISAGE and MAGNET models.

Structural change is an important driver for productivity growth, given the realisation of scale effects and the redistribution of production resources from low-productivity to high-productivity farm operations (Kimura and Sauer, 2015). Numerous factors are listed in the literature as driving this structural change, including labour-saving technological change; relative prices between labour and capital; market requirements – including from processing and distribution systems - related to product safety, quality and product homogeneity; economies of scale; changing demographics; changing work habits and others (National Research Council, 2001). While some of these are likely to more or less continue past trends, e.g. demographic changes, with aging populations linked to low or even negative population growth; technological changes; and requirements for product safety, others will depend on developments that can be markedly different across scenarios, such as market demand for product homogeneity versus short supply chains favouring local and regional markets and potentially smaller farms.

While farm incomes are expected to rise in all scenarios, the share of primary agriculture in overall GDP is bound to decline further over the coming decades, particularly in a *Fast* world. This development is mirrored by a continued reduction of the sector's share in global employment, which is estimated to have shrunk from some 40% in 1994 to just over 30% in 2010. Model results suggest that the agricultural labour share within the global economy is bound to be roughly halved between 2010 and 2050 in the *Sustainable* scenario – more than that foreseen within the *Fast* scenario – while the reduction would be limited to one-third in the *Individual* scenario. This further decline in the agricultural labour share hence represents a continuation of trends observed in the past, although dampened (*Individual*) or accelerated (*Fast*), depending on the scenario. For the *Sustainable* scenario in particular, the extent of this decline will significantly depend on technological choices: to the extent that the reduced use of variable inputs such as synthetic fertilisers and pesticides is compensated for by increased labour use, the decline in agricultural labour use could be slower than suggested by the model results.

For the majority of regions, total labour input in primary agriculture is declining in all three scenarios. Nevertheless, the speed of decline differs both across scenarios – with more modest declines in an *Individual* world and most significant declines in a *Fast* world – and between the two CGE models, depending on the assumed substitutability between labour and other production factors, capital in particular. Agricultural employment in the United States, for instance – which represented about 1.6% of total US employment in 2010 – is shown to fall by between a fourth and a third by 2050, while that in the European Union – which recently totalled about 5% of total EU employment – would fall by between a third and one-half. Given continued population growth and hence increased labour force overall, the development in agricultural employment may be different in Oceania, with little change simulated for the *Individual* scenario and much more modest declines in the other scenarios when compared to the United States or the European Union.

In developing countries, higher population growth and the continued importance of the agricultural sector within the overall economy leads to a less pronounced drop in agricultural employment. Agricultural employment in Sub-Saharan Africa may indeed rise slightly in the medium-term towards 2030 and, for the *Individual* scenario, even more significantly thereafter, to end some 50% higher than today. Even if the agricultural share of the region's total employment falls by at least a third, these results suggest that primary agriculture plays an important role in the creation of economic growth and jobs in this region.

Where do workers move who are no longer employed in farming? In all regions, labour migration away from primary agriculture is accompanied by labour movements away from food processing and the forestry sector (Figure 2.3).[5] All regions show an expanding service sector, attracting labour from other parts of the economy. In the industrialised countries of Europe, North America and Oceania in particular, the service sector will therefore need to absorb the majority of workers who are no longer employed in agriculture and forestry. Other manufacturing sectors may also expand their labour use beyond such a proportional growth, at least in developing countries where the manufacturing industry is still in development. In developed countries, but also in Brazil, there is a relative decline in labour use within the manufacturing sector, although this is much less pronounced than for the land-based sectors.

These findings are relatively stable across the three contextual scenarios, although their magnitudes differ. Generally, the stronger outflow of labour from primary agriculture – and, indeed, agriculture-related sectors in general – found within the *Fast* scenario is associated with higher inflows to the other manufacturing and service sectors. Relative flows tend to be smaller in the *Individual* scenario. Note that the influx of labour to the extractive sector is smallest in the *Sustainable* scenario, consistent with the assumption that there is greater societal focus on sustainable behaviour and notably on lower use of fossil resources.

The declining labour input within primary agriculture is strongly linked to productivity growth in crop and livestock production, particularly where technological change focuses on labour productivity and labour savings. Such changes go in line with rising labour incomes, which are shown by both CGE models to be significant for the coming decades. Similar to employment, the results of the two models show large differences depending on the assumed substitution between labour and other factors and different assumptions on labour mobility across sectors: agricultural wage increases found by the ENVISAGE model, with full labour mobility, are generally higher than those found by MAGNET, which assumes segregation of agricultural and non-agricultural labour markets. The latter model finds a lower agricultural wage growth than in other sectors. General results are similar, however: global average labour wages could more than triple between 2010 and 2050 in a *Fast* world and could still double in the *Individual* scenario. In line with overall income growth, gains in labour incomes are more pronounced in Asia and Latin America than in industrialised countries: on average across the two CGE models, agricultural wages are found to increase between three- and five-fold in Asia and between 2.2- and 3.6-fold in Latin America. Wage growth in Africa is dampened by growth in the agricultural labour force, with increasing average wages between 40% and 190%, while wages in Europe, North America and Oceania could roughly double by 2050. In all cases, wage increases are highest in the *Fast* scenario and lowest in the *Individual* one.

These averages across regions and years hide significant differences across individual farms, which will need to adapt to the changing and volatile environment. This includes natural factors, such as climate change-related risks or requirements to ensure proper pest and disease control, given increased trade and livestock production, but also higher demands for product safety, quality and possibly process characteristics. Both areas develop differently across the three scenarios and are likely to affect different farmers in different ways, depending on regional characteristics and their integration within specific supply chains.

Figure 2.3. Labour migration across sectors, selected developing (upper panel) and developed countries (lower panel), 2050

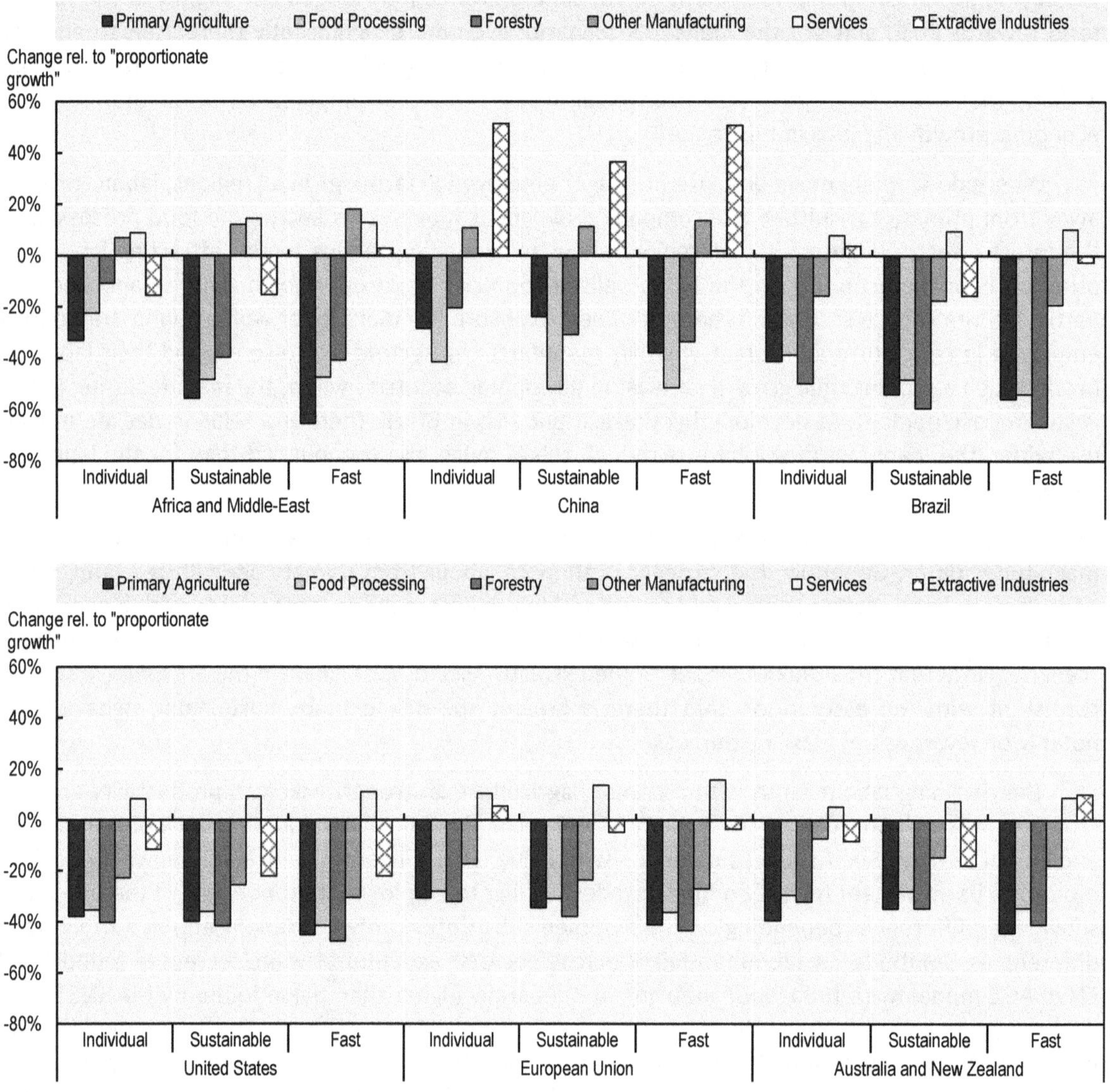

Note: Figures show changes in the labour use simulated for 2050 relative to a hypothetical situation of labour use in all sectors growing proportionally to the regional labour markets. It therefore abstracts from changes to the overall labour markets, which are linked directly to population growth, and only shows the effects of labour migration.

Source: Calculated from MAGNET results.

Biodiversity and scarcities of natural resources

Scarcities and the declining quality of natural resources, such as water, soils and biodiversity, have raised increased interest in developments in food and agriculture, both due to the dependency of agricultural production systems on these resources and to the impacts which increased agricultural production may have on ecosystems. The expansion and intensification of agricultural land use has been among the key factors behind terrestrial biodiversity loss in the past. With demand for agricultural products expanding, land use for crops and agriculture in general is bound to increase further, while natural habitats may remain under pressure.

Indeed, model results suggest that, driven by growing demand, agricultural land use expansion may accelerate relative to past decades (Figure 2.4), unless productivity increases more strongly than assumed in these scenarios. This is particularly the case in African regions, where substantial land reserves are identified but growth in agricultural land use since 1970 has been comparatively slow. The result is a further decline in forest cover: between 2010 and 2050, some 15% of forest could be lost in Sub-Saharan Africa and 4% globally, unless major efforts are undertaken to protect sensitive areas, as shown in both the *Individual* and *Fast* scenarios. In contrast, the *Sustainable* scenario involves greater consumer awareness of the environmental footprint of their food basket. The resulting lower demand for meat and other livestock products frees up significant amounts of resources and halts deforestation to a large extent: in this world, forests in Sub-Saharan Africa would decline by only 12% by 2050, while global forest cover would, after a medium-term drop, recover to 99% of today's forest surface – albeit with changes in regional distribution. All scenarios witness expanded forest cover in a number of developed regions, Europe and North America in particular.

The expansion in agricultural land use is mirrored by increasing requirements for crop land, which tends to be used more intensively than pasture area. Global crop area could increase by up to 18%, while crop land in Sub-Saharan Africa is modelled to increase by between one-third and two-thirds during the 2010-2050 period, depending on scenarios and models (see Figure B.12 in Annex B). In some regions, the *Sustainable* scenario is characterised by particularly rapid crop land expansion: here, global demand is lower for ruminant meat such as beef, which in several regions is pasture-based. Similarly, demand for high-energy staple crops with comparatively low nutritional value is also reduced. Instead, consumption shifts towards higher-value vegetal food, which requires additional crop land. African crop area expansion in the *Sustainable* scenario therefore exceeds that of a *Fast* world, at the expense of pasture land.

As a consequence, natural habitats – including, but not limited to, pristine forests – remain under continued pressure, while the intensification of agricultural production systems is likely to continue to threaten biodiversity through a variety of factors. These include the importance of agricultural production systems in fresh-water withdrawal, which affects biodiversity through water table depletion, salinisation and the reduced availability or quality of surface water further downstream. The use of insecticides is quoted to be responsible for the decline of both insect populations and of those of wild birds and other animals (FAO, 2013), while aquatic ecosystems and fisheries in particular are disturbed by the high use of synthetic fertilisers, manure and leguminous crops (Canfield et al., 2010).

Figure 2.4. Agricultural and forest land cover, 1970-2050: World total and selected regions

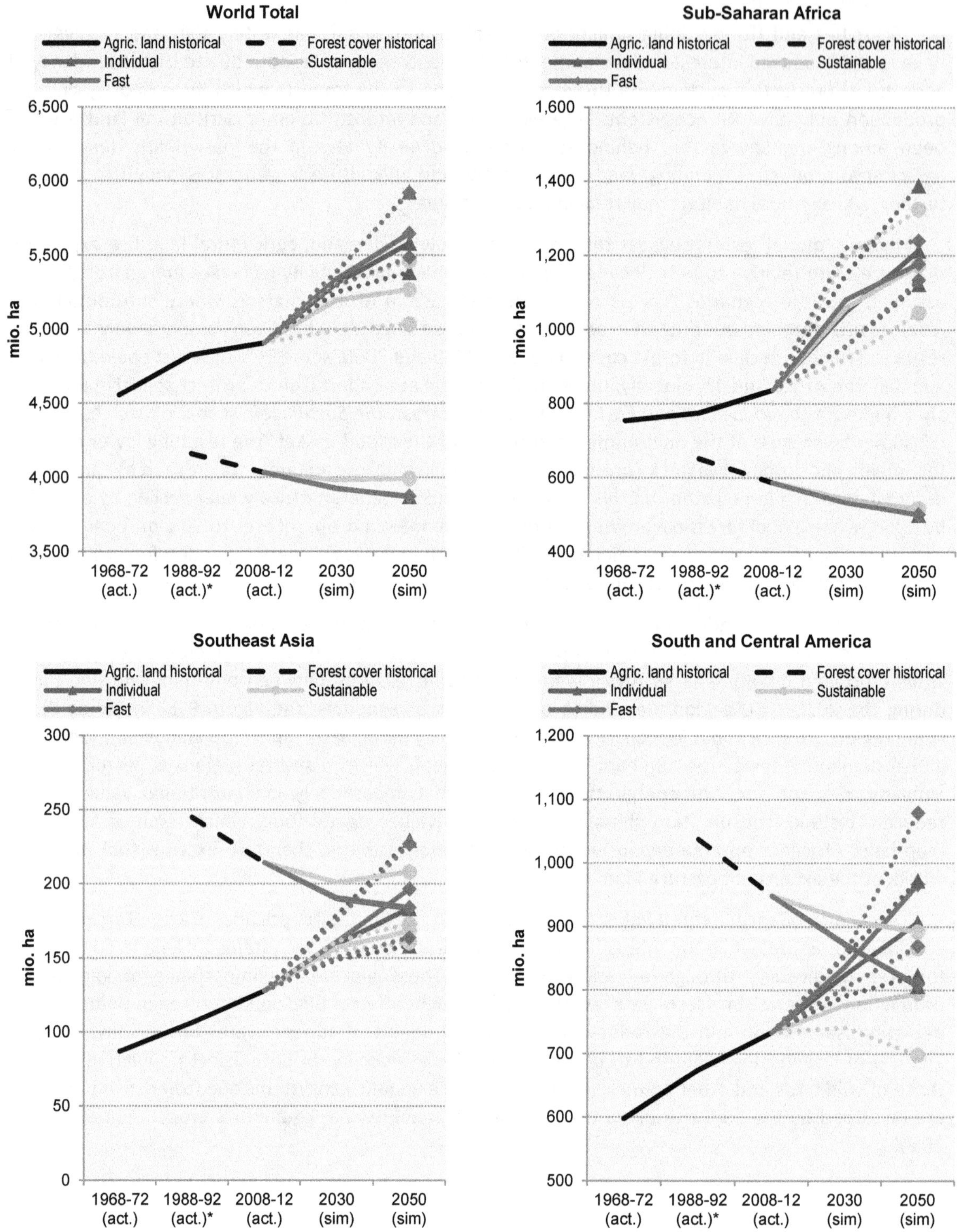

World Total

Sub-Saharan Africa

Southeast Asia

South and Central America

Note: Model results are relative changes in time between 2010, 2030 and 2050, superimposed on actual data from other sources, therefore prospects in levels are derived from additional calculations. Thick lines represent means across the three models providing agricultural land use data, while dotted lines represent the range of model results (minima and maxima). Projections on forest area provided by GLOBIOM only.

* Historical forest data for 1990-92 only.

Source: Historical data from FAOSTAT (2014); prospects from results provided by contributing models.

The OECD estimates that the mean species abundance may fall by a further 10% globally between 2010 and 2050, with the strongest declines in biodiversity found for scrublands and savannahs, temperate forests and tropical forests. Climate change accounts for an increasing share in future biodiversity losses: almost 40% of losses in global mean species abundance between 2030 and 2050 are estimated to be attributed directly to this factor (OECD, 2012). The report also notes that biodiversity loss may have severe implications for economic systems, human well-being and security. While damages related to fisheries or pollination also directly affect OECD countries, the majority of the costs would need to be borne by developing countries, as their total wealth depends on natural capital to a much larger degree (World Bank, 2006). Implications include negative effects on eco-tourism, climate change, due to the role of biodiversity in both climate change mitigation and adaptation; water, including water purification, flow regulation and others; and human health and wellbeing (OECD, 2012).

Water shortages pose a major threat to agriculture, other sectors and households alike. By 2050, some 3.9 billion people could live in areas with severe water stress – a significant increase from 1.6 billion in 2000 (OECD, 2012). South Asia, the Middle East and large parts of the People's Republic of China (hereafter "China") are most affected, while the situation might improve somewhat in several OECD countries. Developments will depend on several factors, including climate change and related changes in precipitation and temperatures, and water use technologies both within agriculture and in other sectors, as well as economic growth.

Given the land use and intensification trends in the three scenarios, one can derive some modification in the threats to biodiversity. The *Individual* and *Fast* scenarios reveal a continuation or even an acceleration of increased land use change and high input use, adding to pressures on habitats and ecosystems. While the model results do not allow the precise quantification of such damage, it appears plausible to expect these two scenarios to amplify the negative developments already observed. In contrast, however, the *Sustainable* scenario features significantly lower pressure on natural resources, including on land use and the discharge of harmful substances such as fertilisers and pesticides. As a consequence, natural habitats and ecosystems are more likely to be preserved in this scenario. Although trends in agricultural area expansion are generally not reversed but instead merely decelerate, a notable exception is Brazil, where the declining demand for ruminant meat could indeed reduce total use of agricultural land and stabilise sensitive areas in the longer run.

Agricultural greenhouse gas emissions and other pollution

While the growth of biomass is a major sink for GHG emissions, agricultural production also accounts for a significant share of global GHG emissions. In 2010, about 65% of emissions in agriculture originated from livestock production, of which almost half were from ruminant meat production alone. Emissions from rice production – methane from the rice fields and nitrous oxides from mineral fertilisers – accounted for about one-fifth of total agricultural emissions (GLOBIOM database, IIASA).

Model results suggest that global emissions from agriculture could significantly increase in all scenarios between 2010 and 2050 (Figure 2.5). Overall emissions are found to increase by 52% in the *Individual* scenario, and by 55% in the higher-growth *Fast* world. This growth in agricultural emissions is driven by the strong increase in overall output. Nevertheless, emission intensities are reduced in several agricultural sectors, including the production of ruminant meat. These improvements depend on various technological developments, notably with respect to livestock feeding and breeds.

Consistent with a more sustainable lifestyle, the *Sustainable* scenario is associated with much lower, albeit still growing, agricultural emissions. These reductions are linked to lower production volumes overall, related to slower population growth as well as to the shift in food consumption patterns, and hence in the agricultural production structure. Critically, this implies healthier and more sustainable diets in the developed world in particular, resulting in reduced consumption – and hence production – of ruminant meat and other livestock products.[6] As a consequence, total emissions from ruminant meat production could shrink by about 6% between 2010 and 2050 in the *Sustainable* world (Figure 2.5).

Figure 2.5. Global agricultural greenhouse gas emissions, 2010 to 2050

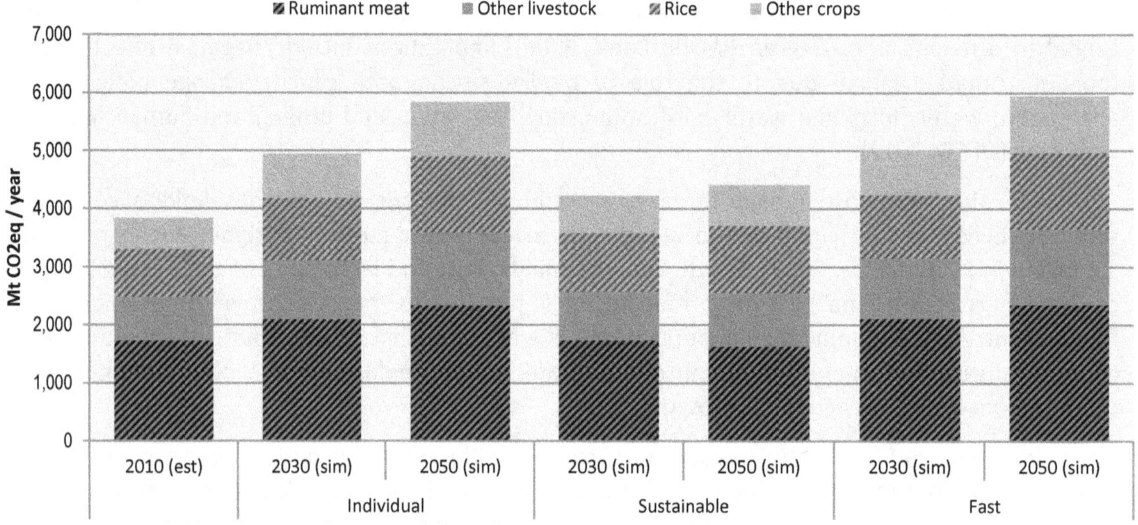

Source: Results on emissions provided by the GLOBIOM model.

These results, however, relate to *direct* agricultural emissions only. Emissions from land use changes would also contribute to the total. As discussed above, land used for agricultural production expands particularly in the *Fast* and *Individual* scenarios, thus potentially affecting carbon-rich areas. The *Sustainable* scenario adds less new land, but particularly in parts of Africa and Southeast Asia could still see significant land use change-related emissions.

As emissions of greenhouse gases spread across the globe's atmosphere, the exact source of agricultural emissions has little influence on its global consequences. At the same time, emissions differ regionally, depending on dominant agricultural processes. Thus, differences in emissions across scenarios are driven by important regional characteristics. Globally, under all contextual scenarios, emissions from livestock products increase slightly less rapidly than those from crops, but given their lion's share in current emissions, livestock production contributes most to the growth in agricultural emissions (Figure 2.6). This also holds for most regions. Emissions from agricultural production – led by livestock systems – are found to rise strongly in developing countries, particularly in the *Individual* and *Fast* scenarios. In contrast, the *Sustainable* world is characterised by more balanced diets, and hence features lower meat consumption by wealthier consumers. Hence, emissions from livestock production in Asia and Latin America – as well as in Europe – may indeed shrink in this scenario. The majority of other regions are also found to have much lower growth in livestock-induced emissions in the *Sustainable* scenario when compared to the other scenarios. In Sub-Saharan Africa, however, the differences are rather small, as reduced emissions from ruminant meat are largely offset by rapidly growing emissions from other livestock, notably dairy and poultry – a consequence of diets moving towards protein from these sources.

Figure 2.6. Regional trends in agricultural greenhouse gas emissions, 2010 to 2050

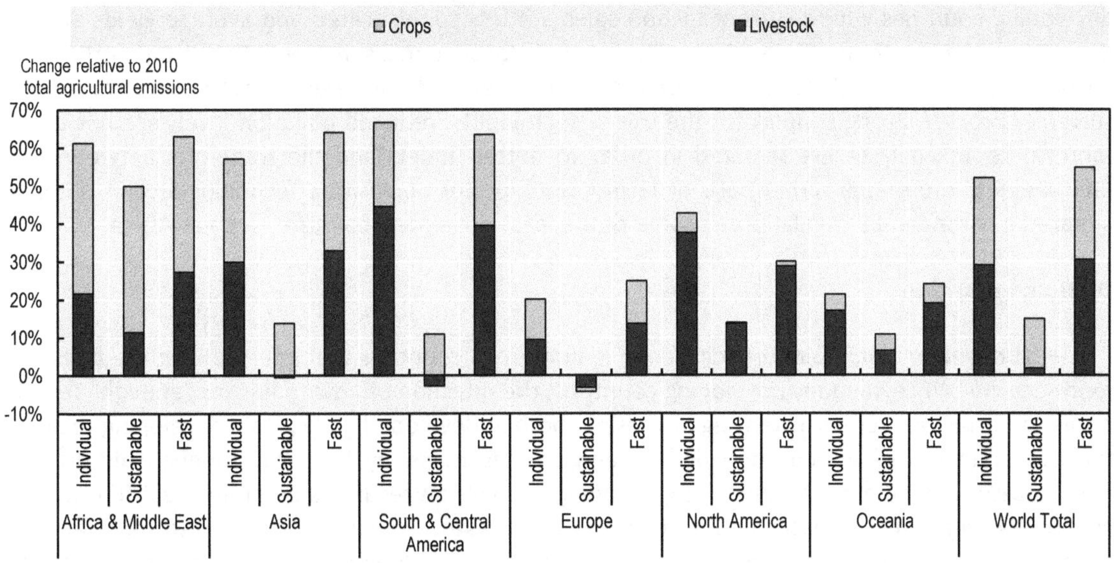

Source: Results on emissions provided by the GLOBIOM model.

Emissions from crop production grow faster than emissions from livestock systems, both globally and in virtually all regions and across scenarios. Average emission intensities – the total emissions per unit of production – for livestock production differ between grazing and mixed systems (Havlik et al., 2014, and in particular Figure S2 of the supporting information provided there). As livestock production develops, meat production shifts from grazing towards mixed and grain-based systems. As a consequence, emission intensities are found to improve by between 25% and 28% globally for ruminant meat. Due to larger shares of grazing systems in the *Sustainable* scenario, improvements in emission intensities are moderately lower than in the two more intensive scenarios. In contrast, improvements through changes in production systems are more modest for most crops. Much of the growth in crop production therefore directly translates into higher emissions.[7]

Other pollutants are also important, even if the models deployed do not offer specific quantitative insights on these. These concern for instance the application of fertilisers, both mineral and organic, and of pesticides. Here again, it is useful to distinguish between pollution intensities – i.e. the amount of pollutants set free per unit of production output – and the scale effects. The development of pollution intensities generally depends on the application intensity of these inputs, the technology used to apply these, and the average yields of the crops. Application intensities of fertilisers and pesticides vary widely across countries: in African countries, fertiliser use per hectare is well below that in the developed world (FAOSTAT, 2014). An intensification of fertiliser use can therefore be seen as a prerequisite to boost land productivity in Africa. In contrast, several countries in Asia, India and Indonesia included, provide strong support in order to reduce fertiliser prices paid by farmers (von Lampe et al., 2014). As a consequence, application rates in these countries are comparatively high and are likely to decline as policies adjust. Finally, application rates in most developed countries could decline slightly in the future, as regulations, concerning fertiliser application and crop requirements, for example, are further developed to address the detrimental environmental effects of fertiliser and technologies. Similar arguments may hold for pesticides, although data availability is much less systematic.

Both application technologies and crop yields can be expected to improve, notably in many developing countries where current technologies are less sophisticated and average yields are lower than what they potentially could be. The overall consequences for pollution from fertiliser and pesticide use are difficult to assess, yet for most developed countries, as well as for those which currently provide strong support for the use of such inputs, reduced pollution levels are not unlikely. More in-depth analyses are required in order to better understand the trade-offs between higher (and, indeed, more appropriate) use of farm inputs, better application technologies and potentially adapted environmental regulations in some of the least-developed countries such as Africa.

Diets and nutrition

Past developments point to a challenge in numerous countries that goes beyond the question of food security. While, in many developing countries, the question of how to ensure "enough" food is of prime importance, there is increasing discussion, both in developed and certain developing regions, of the consequences of options provided to and choices made by food consumers. This discussion encompasses a number of diverse issues, including: i) concerns regarding emerging health trends, such as non-communicable diseases related to excessive intake of sugar or fat, but also meat and meat products,[8] particularly – although not solely – in the more developed countries; ii) the sustainability of consumption patterns driving agricultural and food production; and iii) social developments linked to food consumption, e.g. the social cohesion effects of changing trends in the collective preparation and consumption of meals.

A major caveat to the discussion of food consumption patterns relates to the data foundation. Data on actual food consumption is available only on a partial, fragmented, often dated and generally incomparable basis across countries and regions. As a consequence, a discussion of trends in food consumption patterns, diets and nutrition at international level is generally based on the proxy use of "food availability". It should be noted, however, that data on food availability, as derived for instance from food balance sheets, can substantially deviate from findings of, say, individual dietary surveys (Kearney, 2010).

In general terms, the nutrition transition is described to occur in two stages. These involve, firstly, the "expansion" of food consumption, which is primarily focused on increasing food energy supplies, with the majority of additional calories being derived from cheaper, vegetable feedstuffs. This development has been visible in almost all regions and is largely independent from cultures, religions, traditions and similar factors. The second, "substitution", stage involves a shift in food consumption from away from carbohydrate-rich staples towards vegetable oils, sugar and animal products, largely keeping total energy supplies unchanged. This latter development is much more influenced by culture or religion, and hence develops differently across countries and regions (Schmidhuber and Shetty, 2005, and others).

The composition of food baskets is likely to continue changing over time (Figure 2.7). Given that much of the "substitution" stage of the nutrition transition has already taken place in most industrialised countries, and that growth in per capita incomes in developing and transition economies generally exceed those in developed ones, these changes are expected to be most pronounced in the developing world. Income growth and relative price changes are the key drivers behind this substitution in both the *Individual* and the *Fast* scenarios, resulting in higher shares of livestock products, sugar and vegetable oils, but reduced cereal shares. The decline in the cereal share is most pronounced in China and in South Asia, where rice shares shrink due to rising incomes and other factors.

Consumption patterns are shown to change less significantly in Latin America for these two scenarios, although the share of livestock products – mainly non-ruminant meat such as poultry –

could increase by up to three percentage points between 2010 and 2050, replacing, to a significant degree, staples such as potatoes and dry pulses. While North America and Oceania are also found to slightly increase livestock shares, the average European consumer's calorie share coming from meat and dairy products could fall – although the changes are found to be very small.

Given the focus on more balanced and sustainable diets in the *Sustainable* scenario, the composition of food baskets changes quite differently and more significantly in this world. In developed countries, but also in China and parts of Latin America, this predominantly translates into reduced consumption of livestock products. In South and Southeast Asia, meat shares in average diets would continue to increase, albeit at lower rates compared to the other scenarios, as levels of meat consumption are relatively low. A similar development is found for Sub-Saharan Africa, where the share of staples such as potatoes and cassava is reduced in favour of both meat and grains.

Figure 2.7. Changes in the composition of food availability, 2010 to 2050

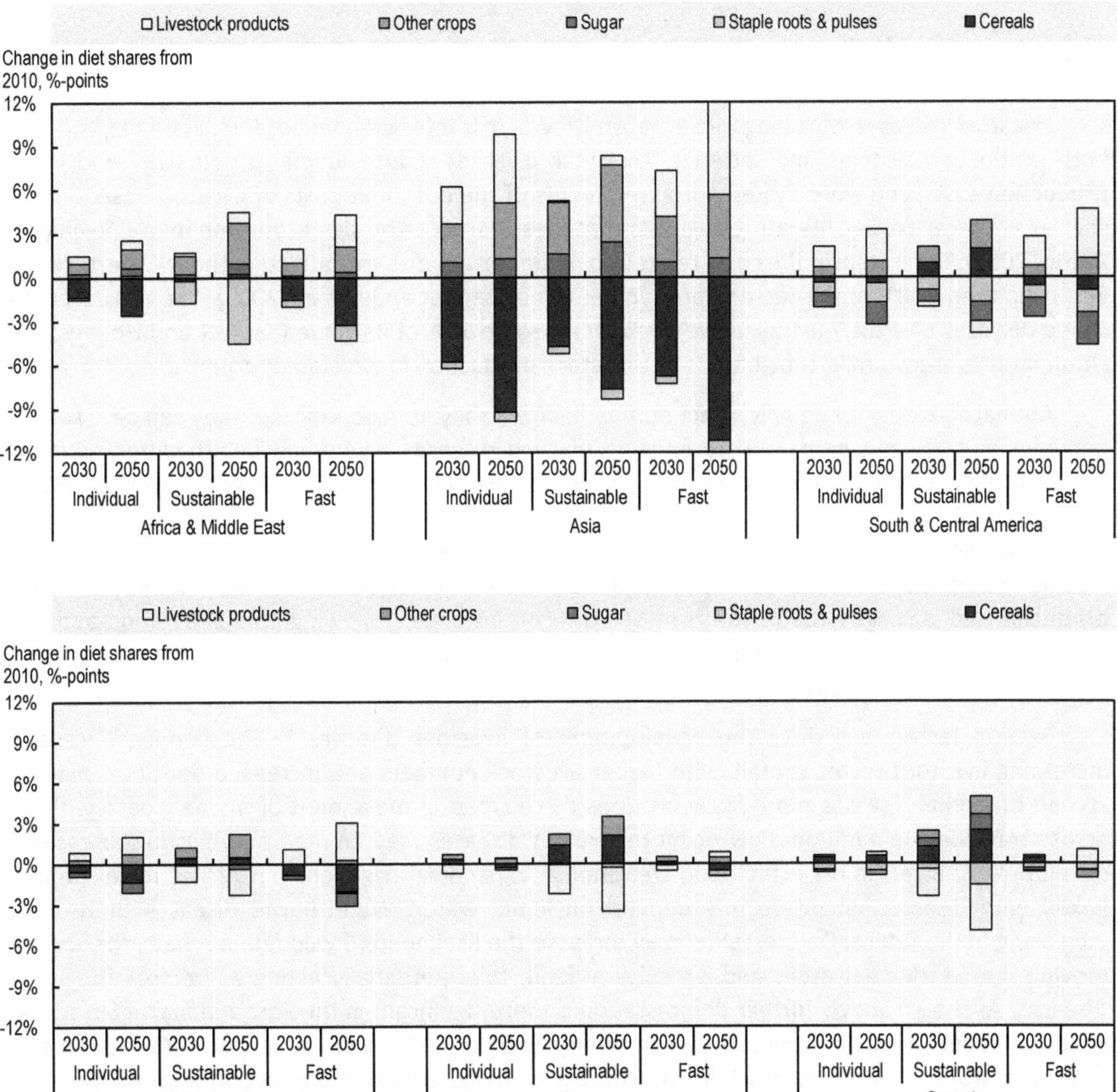

Note: Staple roots & pulses in GLOBIOM include potatoes, sweet potatoes, cassava, chick peas and dry peas.

Source: Results on calorie availability by commodity provided by the GLOBIOM model.

These results from the GLOBIOM model are broadly shared by the second partial equilibrium model IMPACT, which also provides product-specific data on calorie availability. The product coverage is not the same between the two models, causing differences across product categories. This strongly shows for fruits and vegetables, of which IMPACT has a more complete coverage, and for which the average shares are found to increase in all three scenarios (this product group is quite responsive to higher incomes), but most significantly in a *Sustainable* world, as it is also considered to contribute to more balanced diets.

Based on these results, deriving clear conclusions on health and environmental effects is not immediately possible. Nonetheless, one can identify a significant risk of increased prevalence of nutrition-related, non-communicable diseases, notably for the *Individual* and *Fast* scenarios, which are driven by income growth and where the little attention which is paid to balanced and sustainable diets is reflected in the increased intake of meat, fat and sugar in many regions. This is not the case in the *Sustainable* scenario, however, due to the defining trend towards more balanced and sustainable diets, as shown by lower shares of livestock products, among others.

Trans-boundary livestock diseases

Livestock diseases, including those transmitted across international borders, are a major threat to both production systems and societies. Livestock diseases reduce animal productivity and increase production costs, and while systematic assessments of the economic costs of livestock diseases across species are rare, existing literature suggests that these costs can be significant (Innamura, Rushton and Antón, 2015). For instance, the costs related to 32 important diseases afflicting the UK livestock sector was estimated at 8% of the sector's production value (Bennet and Ijplaar, 2005). The top 21 beef and sheep diseases cost the Australian livestock sector some 16% of its value (Sackett and Holmes, 2006). Other studies show similarly high costs for livestock production in developing countries.

Animal diseases can equally affect *human health* if they are zoonotic, i.e. they can be transmitted between animals and humans. The impacts of such diseases on human health differ significantly between high- and low-income countries. In 59 low-income countries zoonoses have been found to cause 13% of the infectious disease burden. In contrast, they represent only 1% of the infectious disease burden in rich countries (Grace et al., 2012). Other indirect effects of animal disease may include uncertainty among consumers, negative effects with respect to the exportability of livestock products, and damages to the tourism sector. For instance, following the 2001 food-and-mouth disease outbreak in the United Kingdom, tourism was the worst-affected sector, with estimated costs of GBP 7.7 billion (IFAH, 2012).

Several factors will drive the development of livestock diseases in the coming decades. An increasing livestock sector overall, with higher livestock numbers and increased densities, makes the spread of animal diseases more likely, as does the increasing movement of animals both within and across countries. In addition, new or more virulent diseases may emerge and existing diseases may develop resistance against established treatments. Expanding irrigation – in Africa, for example – is linked with diseases where vectors depend on liquid water. Water-borne diseases therefore risk increasing in the future. Deforestation may increase the likelihood of wild fauna – bats, for example – moving into settlement areas and agricultural land, thus potentially acting as vectors for livestock diseases. As shown above, further deforestation is more significant in the *Fast* and *Individual* scenarios – with relatively small differences between them – than in the *Sustainable* scenario. At the same time, a move towards housing livestock in the context of more intensive production systems can reduce potential contact with wild animal disease reservoirs or the transmission to humans. Other factors potentially affecting the development and spread of livestock diseases include the conditions characterising the large urban livestock production, processing, marketing and consumption in developing countries' growing cities, while the impact of climate change on the distribution of diseases remains unclear.

At the same time, historical trends suggest that livestock diseases may, overall, *decrease* in importance in industrialised countries. Three factors could be behind this development: i) the gradually improved control of the main epidemic diseases through eradication campaigns; ii) better controls of livestock products at international borders and the increased use of risk assessment to reduce the entry of livestock diseases; and iii) overall improvements in infrastructure, hygiene and animal health inputs.

The three scenarios differ in their exposure to trans-boundary livestock diseases, due to the level and implied density of animal production, the intensity of international trade and the degree of international co-operation. Given the lower reliance on inter-regional trade, animal – as well as crop – diseases tend to remain more limited in their regional coverage in an *Individual* world. At the same time, the rapidly growing production of livestock products and limited international co-operation on prevention and control systems in this scenario result in potentially rapid-spreading and serious impacts within countries and regions.

Strong income growth also drives the strong growth of livestock production in the *Fast* scenario. In addition, increased international and inter-regional trade allows diseases to travel easily across borders and continents. The strong focus on international collaboration which is embedded in this scenario needs to result in enhanced and efficient co-operation on the prevention, rapid identification and control of these diseases. In contrast, the *Sustainable* scenario focuses on lower livestock consumption and production overall. Together with reduced inter-regional trade, higher diversity of species produced in agriculture and increased overall biodiversity, this should limit inter-regional disease spill-overs.

Food safety

Similar to livestock diseases, food safety risks are likely to increase with international food trade. In addition, longer food chains, spreading across countries and continents, may make it harder to ensure the full traceability and safety of ingredients to food products. This, together with the highly input-intensive agricultural production systems, may increase food safety pressures in the *Fast* world. In this scenario, required food safety controls may be partly taken over by multinational food companies and facilitated by largely homogeneous food supplies and enhanced international co-operation.

While the lower relevance of inter-regional trade somewhat dampens these threats in the *Individual* scenario, high input use, increased pollution and possible non-compliance with existing regulation – particularly in times of food shortages – may result in higher risks to food safety in this world. Reduced food safety pressures may be expected for the *Sustainable* scenario, given lower input use and higher levels of biodiversity overall. Some additional risks may evolve from wider diversity in food products if food safety norms are not adequately addressed.

The relative importance of challenges across scenarios

Aggregating the relative importance of individual challenges is difficult and necessarily depends on weights given to each of these. When considering each of the challenges across scenarios, however, it is possible to derive some synthesis, which is attempted in Figure 2.8. Broadly speaking, the *Individual* scenario is characterised by a range of moderate to strong risks across a variety of threats. This scenario can in many aspects be understood as a business-as-usual case, where major concerns present and visible today continue and intensify in the future. Improvements to global food insecurity are limited, with both hunger and overweight continuing to threaten a large number of countries and their health systems. Food safety and animal health are at risk due to high input use in agriculture and little international co-operation in preventing and controlling the spread of harmful substances and organisms within the food chain. Biodiversity losses, agricultural greenhouse gas emissions and pollution risk continue largely unchecked. Given that agricultural prices may no longer be falling in real terms, prospects for farmer incomes and, more broadly, the economic sustainability of farming, are somewhat less of a concern, provided that there are no new and additional barriers to structural change.

The *Sustainable* scenario tends to score better in many areas. Diet-related health problems would be significantly reduced, due to consumer focus on sustainable food baskets and a limitation of ruminant and other meat intake.[9] Food safety and trans-boundary disease-related problems are limited due to reduced agricultural input use and lower overall production intensities, as well as greater biodiversity, although risks do remain, notably due to the diversity of food products available. The limited growth of ruminant meat production contributes to comparatively low growth in agricultural GHG emissions, even if these developments are not sufficient to reverse the trend of increasing emissions. When compared to the other scenarios, the *Sustainable* scenario appears to generate significant challenges with respect to farmers' needs to adjust to changes in consumer behaviour and to citizens' demands for sustainable production methods and for public goods.

International co-operation in numerous fields positively affects the outcomes of the *Fast* scenario, such as on food safety and the economic sustainability of farming in competitive – i.e. relatively land and capital rich – regions. If unchecked, however, the comparatively fast economic growth and rising incomes foreseen in this scenario generate a number of important threats, notably with respect to environmental and health issues.

Figure 2.8 Relative importance of challenges across scenarios

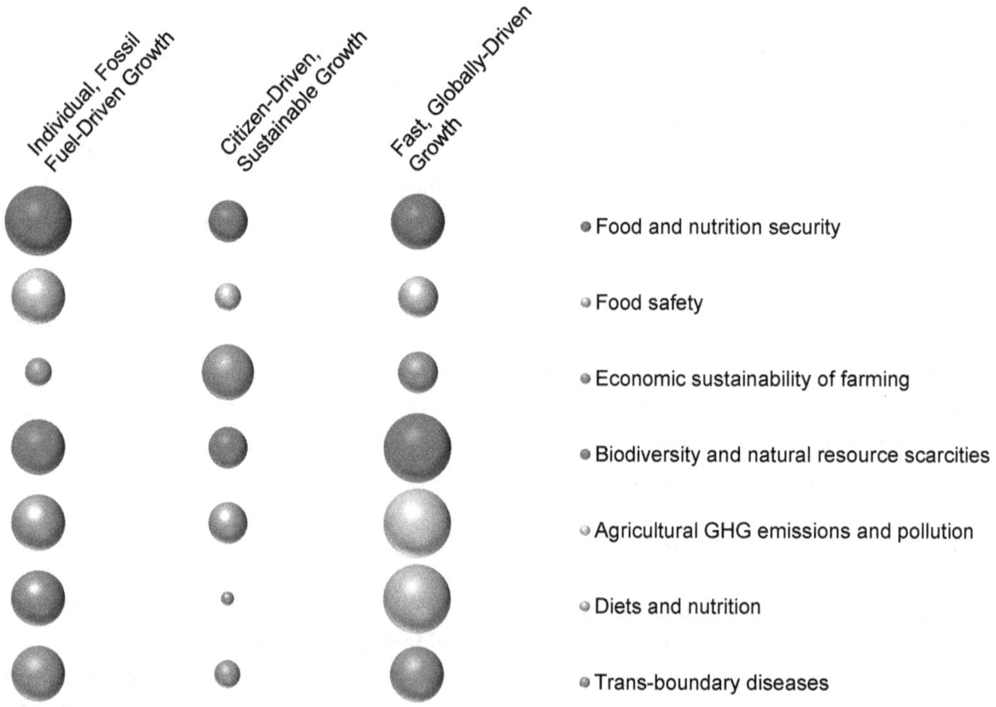

Note: Larger bubbles correspond to greater overall risks related to specific challenges.
Source: Qualitative representation of scenario outcomes, derived from model results and discussions during the scenario workshops.

Notes

1. In a non-representative survey across agricultural ministries of OECD member countries, a total of 26 – partly overlapping – topics were listed as main concerns for strategic thinking on the future of the food and agriculture system. While some of these topics where relatively specific (e.g. the future availability of young farmers for the generational renewal of farms), others were very broad themes (e.g. developing countries). A selection of topics was looked at in greater detail in the work subsequent to the first workshop.

2. Note that the nutritional assumptions for the *Sustainable* scenario have only partially been implemented within IMPACT. See Annex B for more details.

3. The term "structural change" may cover a range of developments within a sector or economy, such as significant changes in the market system or the shift from largely agricultural and rural to more industrialised societies and a growing service sector. The term is used here to describe changes in the number and size distribution of agricultural enterprises.

4. Data have been collected for the years 1930, 1940, etc., to 2000. Generally, however, available data only includes some of these points in time. The data discussed here are from the largest possible time span between 1970 and 2000 and may therefore, where available, comprise between one to four decades.

5. To show labour movements separate from general development in the overall workforce, which itself is largely determined by population growth, the simulated situation for 2050 is compared with a hypothetical situation in which the labour use in all sectors would grow at the rate of total employment. Such changes in sector-specific labour use relative to this "proportionate growth" situation can be interpreted as labour migration across sectors.

6. Scientific evidence links excess meat consumption, red and processed meat in particular, with various non-communicable diseases, including heart diseases, type 2 diabetes, certain cancers and others. See Bender (1992); Kaluza et al. (2012); Pan et al. (2012); World Cancer Research Fund/American Institute for Cancer Research (2007). A more extensive list of references can be found in Johns Hopkins Bloomberg School of Public Health (undated).

7. It should be noted that changes in emission intensities due to improved practices within production systems are not represented here. Improvements in technologies and methods may have the potential to significantly reduce agricultural emissions and would be more likely to be implemented in the *Sustainable* scenario than in the *Fast* or even the Individual scenarios, thus further accentuating the differences in emissions across scenarios.

8. See Note 6.

9. While meat and other animal products can provide an important protein source, excess meat consumption is linked with various non-communicable types of diseases. See endnote 15 for more details and a list of references.

References

Bender, A. (1992), "Meat and Meat Products in Human Nutrition in Developing Countries", *FAO Food and Nutrition Paper* 53, Food and Agriculture Organization, Rome, www.fao.org/docrep/t0562e/t0562e00.htm.

Bennett, R.M. and J. Ijpelaar (2005), "Updated estimates of the costs associated with 34 endemic livestock diseases in Great Britain: A note", *Journal of Agricultural Economics*, Vol. 56, pp. 135-144, United Kingdom, http://onlinelibrary.wiley.com/doi/10.1111/j.1477-9552.2005.tb00126.x/abstract.

Canfield, D.E., A.N. Glazer and P.G. Falkowski (2010), "The evolution and future of Earth's nitrogen cycle", *Science,* Vol. 330, pp. 192-196, American Association for the Advancement of Science, United States, www.sciencemag.org/content/330/6001/192.full.pdf.

FAO (2013), *Aspects Determining the Risk of Pesticides to Wild Bees: Risk Profiles for Focal Crops on Three Continents*, Food and Agriculture Organization, Rome, www.fao.org/uploads/media/risk_pest_wildbees.pdf.

FAO (2010), *World Programme for the Census of Agriculture 2000*, Food and Agriculture Organization, Rome. Reports and comparison tables available from www.fao.org/economic/ess/ess-wca/wca-2000/en (accessed 29 October 2015).

FAO (2009), *Declaration of the World Summit on Food Security*, World Summit on Food Security, 16-18 November 2009, Food and Agriculture Organization, Rome, www.fao.org/fileadmin/templates/wsfs/Summit/Docs/Final_Declaration/WSFS09_Declaration.pdf.

FAO (1996), *Rome Declaration on World Food Security and World Food Summit Plan of Action*, World Food Summit, Rome, 13-17 November 1996, Food and Agriculture Organization, Rome, www.fao.org/docrep/003/w3613e/w3613e00.htm.

FAOSTAT (2014), Statistical Data of the Food and Agriculture Organization website (database), Food and Agriculture Organization, Rome, http://faostat3.fao.org/home/E (accessed 28 November 2014).

Foresight (2010), *Workshop Report: W4 Expert Forum on the Reduction of Food Waste*, The Government Office for Science, London, http://s3.amazonaws.com/zanran_storage/www.bis.gov.uk/ContentPages/2374836301.pdf.

Grace, D. et al. (2012), "The multiple burdens of zoonotic disease and an ecohealth approach to their assessment", *Tropical Animal Health and Production,* Vol. 44/S1, pp. 67-73, Springer, United States, http://doi:10.1007/s11250-012-0209-y.

IFAH (2012), *The Costs of Animal Disease*, report produced for the International Federation for Animal Health, Oxford Analytica, United Kingdom, www.ifahsec.org/white-paper-the-costs-of-animal-disease.

Inamura, M., J. Rushton and J. Antón (2015), "Risk Management of Outbreaks of Livestock Diseases", *OECD Food, Agriculture and Fisheries Papers*, No. 91, OECD Publishing, Paris. DOI: http://dx.doi.org/10.1787/5jrrwdp8x4zs-en].

Johns Hopkins Bloomberg School of Public Health (undated), "Health and environmental implications of U.S. meat consumption and production", Johns Hopkins Center for a Liveable

Future, www.jhsph.edu/research/centers-and-institutes/johns-hopkins-center-for-a-livable-future/projects/meatless_monday/resources/meat_consumption.html (accessed 29 October 2015).

Kaluza, J., A. Wolk and S.C. Larsson (2012), "Red meat consumption and risk of stroke: A meta-analysis of prospective studies", *Stroke*, Vol. 43, pp. 2556-60, http://dx.doi.org/10.1161/strokeaha.112.663286 (accessed 29 October 2015).

Kearney, J. (2010), "Food consumption trends and drivers", *Philosophical Transactions of the Royal Society*, Vol. 365, pp. 2793-2807, http://rstb.royalsocietypublishing.org/content/365/1554/2793.

Kimura, S. and J. Sauer (2015), *Dynamics of Dairy Farm Productivity Growth: Cross-Country Comparison, OECD Food, Agriculture and Fisheries Papers,* No. 87, OECD Publishing, Paris, http://dx.doi.org/10.1787/5jrw8ffbzf7l-en.

National Research Council (2001), *Publicly Funded Agricultural Research and the Changing Structure of U.S. Agriculture*, Committee to Review the Role of Publicly Funded Agricultural Research on the Structure of U.S. Agriculture, National Academy Press, Washington, DC, www.nap.edu/read/10211/chapter/1.

OECD (2012), *OECD Environmental Outlook to 2050: The Consequences of Inaction*, OECD Publishing, Paris, http://dx.doi.org/10.1787/9789264122246-en.

Pan, A. (2012), "Red meat consumption and mortality: Results from two prospective cohort studies", *Archive of Internal Medicine* 172/7, pp. 555-63, http://dx.doi.org/10.1001/archinternmed.2011.2287.

Sackett, D. and P. Holmes (2006), *Assessing the Economic Cost of Endemic Disease on the Profitability of Australian Beef Cattle and Sheep Producers*, Meat and Livestock Australia Limited, North Sydney, www.mla.com.au/Research-and-development/Search-R-D-reports/RD-report-details/R-and-D-Report-Download?itemId=68.

Schmidhuber, J. and P. Shetty (2005), "The nutrition transition to 2030: Why developing countries are likely to bear the major burden", *Acta Agriculturae Scandinavica*, Section C – Food Economics, Vol. 2, Issue 3-4, www.tandfonline.com/doi/abs/10.1080/16507540500534812#.VjlXnrerTC0.

Von Lampe, M. et al. (2014), *Fertiliser and Biofuel Policies in the Global Agricultural Supply Chain*, OECD Food, Agriculture and Fisheries Papers, No. 69, OECD Publishing, Paris, http://dx.doi.org/10.1787/5jxsr7tt3qf4-en.

World Bank (2006), *Where is the Wealth of Nations? Measuring Capital for the 21st Century*, World Bank, Washington D.C., http://documents.worldbank.org/curated/en/2005/12/6623427/wealth-nations-measuring-capital-21st-century.

World Cancer Research Fund / American Institute for Cancer Research (2007), *Food, Nutrition, Physical Activity, and the Prevention of Cancer: A Global Perspective*, AICR, Washington, D.C., www.dietandcancerreport.org/cancer_resource_center/downloads/Second_Expert_Report_full.pdf.

Chapter 3

Policy and implementation strategies for the future of food and agriculture

In spite of the uncertainties which surround the future of food and agricultural systems, there is clarity in one respect: the choices made by policy makers, businesses and consumers today will be pivotal in determining the extent to which global food and agriculture systems will be impacted by the challenges discussed in the previous chapters. This chapter identifies and discusses five key strategies for action by public actors – and indeed other stakeholders, where relevant: i) accelerated movement towards more sustainable lifestyles and consumption patterns, ii) increased coherence of food market regulations, iii) sustainable productivity growth and climate resilience, iv) strengthened infrastructure, and v) improved and broadened risk management systems. The majority of these would enable the management of risks and seizing of opportunities across different scenarios with no or limited side-effects, even if the magnitude of the benefits may vary.

Key strategy areas for policy, industry and society

The future of food and agriculture remains highly uncertain. Nevertheless, even in the absence of precise forecasts and predictions, one thing is clear: decisions taken by policy makers and private actors (such as private companies, farmers, the research community, consumers and civil society) today are likely to affect outcomes in future decades. Policy intervention can take a variety of forms, including measures to accelerate sustainable productivity growth and, more generally, soft approaches to change lifestyles. Private entities can meanwhile complement the work of public bodies in a variety of strategic areas, such as the generation and dissemination of data; consumer awareness-raising; socially responsible investment and the management of risks related to farming. Consumers, for their part, play a role via their purchasing decisions, while citizens influence political processes. Constructive, co-ordinated action between all of these actors is therefore key.

The strategies taken should be holistic, extending beyond the agricultural production sector itself. General economic policies and investments, including macroeconomics, general education, growth policies and broader rural development, can all have significant positive spill-overs for a number of challenges identified above, such as food and nutrition security, for example. This is also evident from comparisons of the Fast, Globally-Driven Growth and Individual, Fossil Fuel-Driven Growth scenarios: international co-operation in various areas, trade and technological developments included, has major implications due to the generation of income opportunities, not least in developing countries.

A second cross-cutting area of engagement needs to be the parallel promotion of sustainability and productivity growth. Agricultural Innovation Systems comprise not just investments in R&D, but also, crucially, include the whole framework of institutions and infrastructure which enable private and public R&D – as well as private-public partnerships – to develop future-proof methods and technologies, test and showcase these developments within the agriculture and food sectors, and ensure their broad and international application.

In particular, five key strategies are identified, not only for policy but also for the private sector, consumers and citizens, where relevant:[1]

- accelerated movement towards more sustainable lifestyles and consumption patterns
- increased coherence of food market regulations
- sustainable productivity growth and climate resilience
- improved infrastructure
- improved and broadened risk management systems.

Each of these are outlined in detail below.

Accelerated movement towards more sustainable lifestyles and consumption patterns

The movement towards more sustainability-oriented lifestyles is a process that is already taking place today in many – mostly developed – countries. As incomes rise, consumers demand "environmental friendliness" as an additional luxury good, in addition to the provision of environmental public goods. In order to further mainstream this focus on environmental, social and economic sustainability, however, a number of joint efforts may be required, ranging from education, e.g. awareness-raising of the consequences of consumption patterns; technology development, e.g. smart fridges; public procurement, e.g. for school and ministry canteens; to regulatory measures, e.g. appropriate food labelling systems. International co-operation is required in many of these areas in order to not only avoid trade frictions arising from differing labelling requirements, but also to account for the increased communication between and ongoing cross-influencing and assimilation of different lifestyles.[2]

Changing lifestyles is a longer-term process, requiring the broad involvement of all stakeholders as well as sufficient flexibility to allow for divergent approaches. Education and "nudging'" are key tools to advance more sustainable lifestyles. Given their more long-term nature, however, other efforts with more short-term impacts are needed, in particular the mainstreaming of sustainable food consumption objectives into policy making across ministries. A number of policy areas have therefore been identified for public sector action, including the following (based on Moomaw et al., 2012):

- A reform of **subsidy and tax systems** could shift incentives away from the production and consumption of resource-intensive and unhealthy food products, away from waste, and towards more sustainable and healthy diets. Several countries have introduced, or are considering introducing, taxes on food which is considered to be unhealthy, such as fatty food or "junk food". While care needs to be taken to appropriately define the disincentives created, such taxes may have positive effects on consumers' diets where demand is price sensitive.
- **Public awareness campaigns** can play a significant role in addressing and curbing unsustainable food consumption. Such campaigns need to be tailored to specific goals and target groups, taking gender and cultural norms surrounding the production and provision of food into account.
- **Regulatory measures** can affect the advertising and marketing of food, the labelling of products or serving sizes. While advertising for alcohol or tobacco is increasingly regulated in numerous countries, there is limited analysis on similar regulations in the food sphere.
- Public authorities purchase large amounts of food for hospitals, schools and other public service organisations. Research has indicated that the incorporation of sustainability dimensions within **public sector food procurement** has led to reduced ecological footprints and the greater engagement of civil society (UNRISD, 2011).

With respect to the private sector, a number of important actions are already being led by business organisations to stimulate innovation, re-orientate relationships between governing actors and consumers, set rules, and monitor compliance enforcement. Some of these opportunities for private sector engagement include the following (based on Moomaw et al., 2012):

- Evidence suggests that retailers can generate greater customer loyalty by enabling consumers to reduce their waste than by lower prices or special offers. When helped by supermarkets to save money by **reducing food waste,** consumers tend to trade-up to higher quality and hence foods with better margins (Foresight, 2010).[3]
- **Voluntary standards and certifications** can help to build brand loyalty, increase consumer awareness and shape consumption patterns. Examples of such standards include the Marine Stewardship Council, Rainforest Alliance or the business-to-business standard GlobalGAP.

A further potential pathway for sustainable food production is the development of alternative food sources. A number of scientific or expert-led explorations are already underway to develop and promote future alternative foods. Granted, some of these ambitions may eventually prove difficult to achieve on a broad basis, or may encounter unanticipated downsides. Nevertheless, they could have the potential to significantly and sustainably improve food availability. While some of these developments, such as saline- or drought-resistant crops, may have little impact on consumers' food experience other than through price effects, others may require dramatic shifts in terms of cultural norms. Examples of such initiatives include:

- **Expanding consumption of low-intensity foodstuffs:** Sometimes called 'mini-meats', **insects** could provide a potentially abundant source of protein (approximately 1 400 species are edible for humans). Suggestions for usage include employing ground insects as filler within processed meat products where mixed-meats are already common either intentionally or through cross-contamination in food processing facilities. While incorporating insects in diets is often presented in western media for its shock value, some populations already consume insects as a regular part of their diet. For example, caterpillars and locusts are popular in Africa, wasps are a delicacy in Japan and crickets are eaten in Thailand. Recent debates have also explored the possibility of using insects as feed for livestock.[4]

- **Opening up new spaces of production:** Scientists suggest that ocean-grown **algae** could open up new tracts of productive space for the growth of food for human consumption – an attractive possibility given the growing population and increased pressures on available land. Already a staple in Asia and Japan, algae is a multifunctional product and, as with insect protein, could also be used in processed foods.[5]

- **New food provenance: Cultured meat** grown in the lab has been discussed in the media for decades, but in 2013, Dutch scientists grew strips of meat from the stem cells of cows, named "test-tube burgers".[6] Initial research was funded by NASA as part of its search for food which astronauts could consume. Proponents of cultured meat suggest that labs may enable precision "lab-farming" with respect to nutritional food characteristics, such as related to its fat content. There are also contested claims that cultured meat may lead to reductions in demand for water and energy while also reducing emissions – providing that these are not offset by energy used to create *in vitro* meat. **Hydroponic vegetable production** is another technology which would potentially enable the production of high-quality, high-yield vegetables with the reduced use of natural resources. Work by the South African Agricultural Research Council suggests savings in water and land use and reductions in pollution.[7]

- **New food composition:** Linked to the concept of personalised nutrition provided by smart sensors and wearable or swallowable technologies is the prediction that new ways of synthesising vitamins and minerals may lead to complete meal replacement liquids. Soylent,[8] a product which claims to be a complete nutritionally-balanced meal in a glass, is one example. The potential use of such products would be for emergency situations or for those with health conditions which prevent them from eating solid food.

A widespread move towards more sustainable and potentially healthier diets, notably when based on less ruminant and other animal protein, would have major implications for overall market developments and outcomes in different domains. Most importantly, the reduced production of meat would enable reductions in the associated use of grazing land and feed crops, and therefore free up significant resources in terms of land and inputs. These resources could not only improve the availability of food for consumers in poor developing countries, but also benefit biodiversity and other environmental variables. In addition, the shift towards nutritionally high-value vegetal food would likely benefit consumer health and national health systems.

A more holistic trend towards sustainability would, however, also include the protection of biodiversity-sensitive areas, and hence the limitation of land available for agricultural production. This approach has its drawbacks: firstly, agricultural production does not necessarily reduce local biodiversity, and secondly, such a restriction would exhibit significant trade-offs as, despite potential reductions in the consumption of animal proteins in high meat consumption countries, the combined effect on food availability would be detrimental for consumers in Africa, Asia and Latin America. Nevertheless, results from the GLOBIOM model suggest that in the Citizen-Driven, Sustainable Growth scenario (hereafter referred to as the "*Sustainable*" scenario for easier reading), the negative effects on calorie availability from a move towards a greener lifestyle[9] would be comparatively small and by 2050 would not exceed 2.3% (in Sub-Saharan Africa). This compares to a 7% reduction in calorie available that such a move would generate in that region in the Individual, Fossil Fuel-Driven Growth scenario (the "*Individual*" scenario in short). This is because agricultural land in the *Sustainable* scenario expands much less into sensitive areas even without specific measures to protect them. In addition, calorie availability levels are higher in the *Sustainable* scenario, making such negative effects more bearable.

A move towards more sustainable diets would also have considerable positive effects in other areas. With the lower consumption and production of livestock products, the risks related to livestock diseases would likely be smaller, as a key driver – the density and proximity of livestock units – would be reduced. Similarly, the emissions of livestock-related greenhouse gases would be reduced by up to 30% in the Fast, Globally-Driven Growth scenario (referred to as the "*Fast*" scenario for brevity). Due to the protection of sensitive areas and consequent reduction of grazing land, livestock-related GHG emissions would also be reduced within the *Sustainable* scenario, although the global effect would be much lower, at 2%.

In contrast, agricultural producers, as well as the food industry, would need to undergo adjustments in order to adapt to changes in consumption patterns and to cope with the reduced availability of sensitive areas for production. This would in particular affect farm operations which are specialised in ruminant meat, in addition to those located in these sensitive areas.

Better **waste management** is another critical element of sustainable consumption. Although determined in part by consumer lifestyles, improved waste management will also involve changes along the entire supply chain. Precise information as to the quantities of agricultural produce lost or wasted between fields and households remains difficult to obtain, and analyses of the underlying causes of and economic requirements for significant changes are scarce. Nevertheless, most stakeholders agree that there is substantial potential for improvements. This also includes the increased use of biomass which is co-produced with food and feed commodities in the context of a growing bio-economy.

Increased coherence of food market regulations

The comparison of the three scenarios shows that international co-operation will play a major role in shaping developments and outcomes in food and agriculture over the coming decades. Importantly, the exchange of goods and services, methods, ideas and technologies, as well as capital and investments, has the potential to raise both incomes and productivity. This has clear benefits for food security, while effects on farmers, biodiversity or GHG emissions are more nuanced.

Differences in food-related regulations have long been identified as hampering international trade in agriculture and food products. While regulations generally help to achieve important policy objectives by responding to a range of societal concerns, often related to market failures, differences in regulations and their enforcement lead to increased costs related to administration, the gathering of information, conformity assessments, etc.

The move towards more compatible and coherent regulations is ongoing at both regional and multilateral levels, including through the international standard-setting bodies Codex Alimentarius (Codex), the International Plant Protection Convention (IPPC) and the World Organization for Animal Health (OIE). Nonetheless, coherence should not be confused with uniformity of standards, as regional and national conditions and consumer and citizens' preferences for protection often differ. In addition, ambitions for more market integration should not conflict with national and international efforts to make agricultural production and the food chain more sustainable. Nevertheless, differences in food regulations may also be based on protectionist motives of governments. The benefits of greater coherence may include better access to markets or foreign products through enhanced international trade, capacity building and knowledge spill-overs, cost reductions for producers and consumers, and improved management options in the case of crises, such as pandemic outbreaks or geopolitical conflicts. While the international standard-setting bodies represent key actors in the development of more coherent regulations, private standards lack democratic backing and may therefore account less for the diverging views of all relevant stakeholders.

Improved international coherence of food market regulations[10] is an important policy area. OECD (2011a) reports that costs in food trade related to non-tariff measures (NTMs) exceed those related to tariffs in seven out of eight economic regions analysed, with India being the sole exception. Tariff equivalents for food-related NTMs are reported to be between 30% and 70%. Given the domestic policy purpose which food regulations have, not all of that is open for reduction, however. There exist various forms of international regulatory co-operation, ranging from better transparency on existing regulation to full harmonisation across countries, covering regulatory procedures and regulations, as well as their implementation and enforcement, and regulators require more clarity as to which mechanisms should be favoured for specific regulatory cases. Separating standards into different "layers" or "modules", e.g. by explicitly building national regulations from international standards and additional requirements where needed, may provide a compromise between the aim of trade cost reductions and the need for regulations which are adapted to the specific contexts within countries.

Reductions in trade costs for agricultural products, through more coherent food market regulations and their implementation, would decrease food prices in importing countries while raising them in exporting countries. Globally, they would contribute to the improved allocation of productive resources across countries and products, raising the overall supply of agricultural and food products. As a consequence, they would help to improve food and nutrition security through higher food availability in importing regions, while raising the economic profitability of farm operations in exporting countries. The magnitude of these effects will differ across scenarios, however, given the different degree of international co-operation and hence different developments in regulation-related trade costs embedded within them. Additional efforts in combatting regulatory heterogeneity are most important in a world with little emphasis on international co-operation per se. Therefore, the gains from such extra efforts are relatively small in the *Fast* scenario.

Model results suggest that a reduction of trade costs through the improvement of regulatory coherence can indeed contribute to food security in developing regions while improving the economic performance in food exporting countries, although differences in the results of the participating models are considerable (Figures 3.1 and 3.2).

The impacts of improved regulatory coherence are most pronounced relative to the *Individual* scenario which, without further policy action, features substantial increases in trade costs, notably between the large regional blocks, and where efforts on regulatory coherence would consequently bring about the largest trade cost reductions. South Africa and Sub-Saharan Africa are found to be the regions which stand to benefit the most: calorie availability could improve by up to 3.3% and 2.4% respectively, depending on the model. Positive effects are also found for the majority of other regions, although these tend to be small. Clearly, the benefits of improved regulatory coherence for food security are most evident in food-importing developing countries. Exporting regions, such as Latin America, experience much less increase in their food availability, as the reductions in trade costs primarily benefit the export sector.

Figure 3.1. Changes in per capita calorie availability due to improved regulatory coherence, 2050

Change relative to no policy

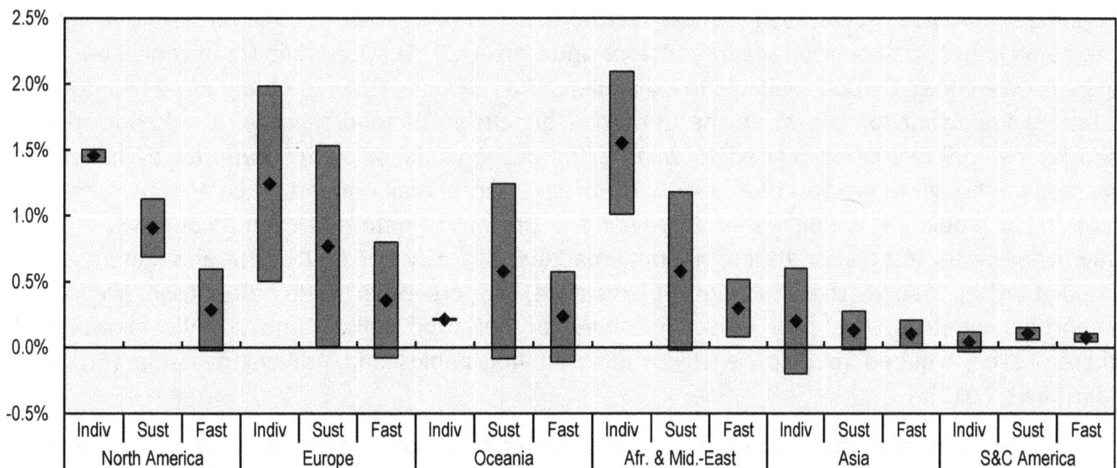

Note: Trade cost reductions within and between the three large world regions are assumed to correspond to 5% and 15% of trade value relative to the Individual, Fossil Fuel-Driven Growth scenario, 10% and 10% relative to the Citizen-Driven, Sustainable Growth scenario, and 5% and 5% relative to the Fast, Globally-Driven Growth scenario, respectively. The three world regions are defined to include the Americas; Europe, Africa and the Middle East; and Asia and Oceania. Changes shown are relative to the respective scenario without policy change. Bars and diamonds indicate ranges and averages across models, respectively.

Source: Results provided by the GLOBIOM and MAGNET models.

Figure 3.2. Changes in regional farm incomes due to improved regulatory coherence, 2050

Change relative to no policy

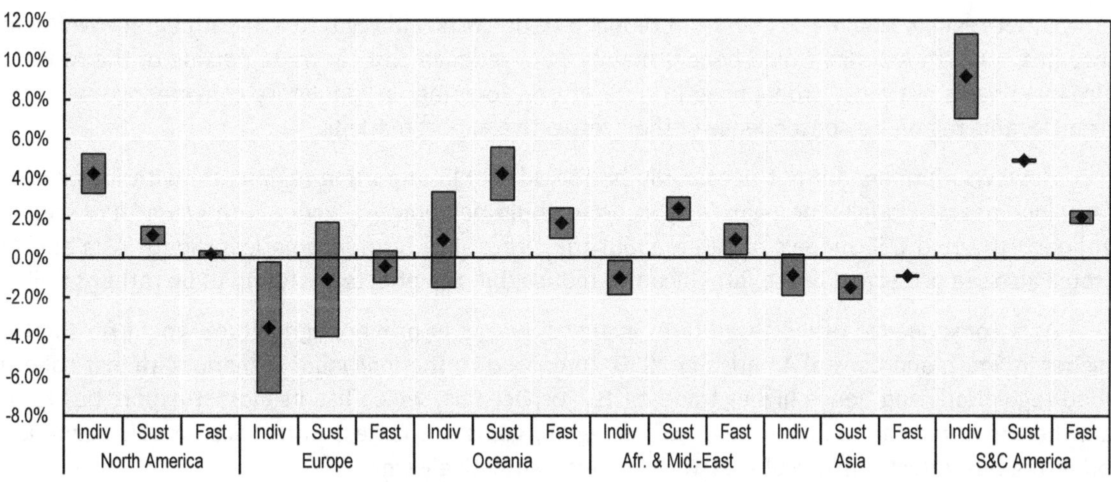

Note: Trade cost reductions within and between the three large world regions are assumed to correspond to 5% and 15% of trade value relative to the Individual, Fossil Fuel-Driven Growth scenario, 10% and 10% relative to the Citizen-Driven, Sustainable Growth scenario, and 5% and 5% relative to the Fast, Globally-Driven Growth scenario, respectively. The three world regions are defined to include the Americas; Europe, Africa and the Middle East; and Asia and Oceania. Changes shown are relative to the respective scenario without policy change.

Source: Results provided by the ENVISAGE and MAGNET models.

The reduction of trade costs has other benefits which are not captured by average calorie availability. A well-functioning trading system has an important role to play in cushioning local and regional supply-side shocks, such as those related to extreme weather or civil unrest, and in mitigating their adverse impacts on food security (Baldos and Hertel, 2015). More fluid trade connections would increase the choice of food available to consumers, thus allowing them to obtain more balanced diets, which is important for improving the utilisation dimension of food security. In addition, domestic shocks, e.g. yield variation related to weather or pests, could be better buffered by international markets, although the exposure to shocks on those international markets, such as those seen in the late 2000s, would also be increased. Finally, it is important to note that even if countries as a *whole* gain from better integration to international markets, this may not be true for all segments of their population, at least in the short-run. For instance, if more open trade raises food availability in importing countries, this may reduce incomes for net food sellers, and specific measures may therefore be required to help negatively-affected households and prevent hardship (Brooks and Matthews, 2015).

South America is the prime beneficiary of lower trade costs when it comes to the economic performance of its farms (Figure 3.2). Within the *Individual* scenario in particular, which by default is characterised by a lack of international co-operation, little focus on coherent food regulations and hence comparatively high trade costs, a reduction of regulatory heterogeneity could increase average farm incomes in South and Central America by around 9% by 2050. Brazil is found to increase average farm incomes by about 12% in that scenario, demonstrating its prominent role as an agricultural exporter. The gain would be less pronounced in the *Sustainable* world, where the focus on trade cost reductions across world regions is smaller compared to trade costs within these regions. Nevertheless, farm incomes could be about 5% higher in 2050 on average for South and Central America.

Other regions would also gain from reduced trade costs, although to a lesser degree. While farm incomes in North America would benefit mainly from reduced costs in trade outside of the Americas, Oceanian gains are most pronounced in their efforts focusing on regulatory convergence within the Asia-Oceania region – a consequence of their respective export markets.

However, farmers are not necessarily better off within importing regions as, with lower prices, farm incomes would fall. European farm incomes could be about 4% lower in the *Individual* scenario, although the two CGE models disagree about the size of the farm income loss. South Asia and Asia would also see prices and hence farm incomes reduce, but the effects are found to be rather small.

As a consequence of increased farm incomes, wages in primary agriculture would be some 3% higher in South and Central America in 2050, compared to the *Individual* scenario with less coherent food regulations and hence higher trade costs. For Oceania, which has its closest export ties to Asia and hence within the assumed large world region, gains are largest in the *Sustainable* scenario. In other regions, effects on agricultural wages would be relatively small.

These model results only provide insights on the average farm. In reality, the heterogeneity of farms within a region, in terms of farm size, production focus and export orientation, to name just a few, ensures that effects on specific operations may diverge from this average. Impacts will differ between crop and livestock producers and indeed, across individual products, given the specific regulatory barriers faced and reduced. Small farms are more likely to face regulatory heterogeneity as an unsurmountable barrier to engagement in export activities. Therefore, efforts to make food regulation more coherent may enable small enterprises to take advantage of export opportunities that would otherwise not exist.

Figure 3.3. Changes in agricultural wages due to improved regulatory coherence, 2050

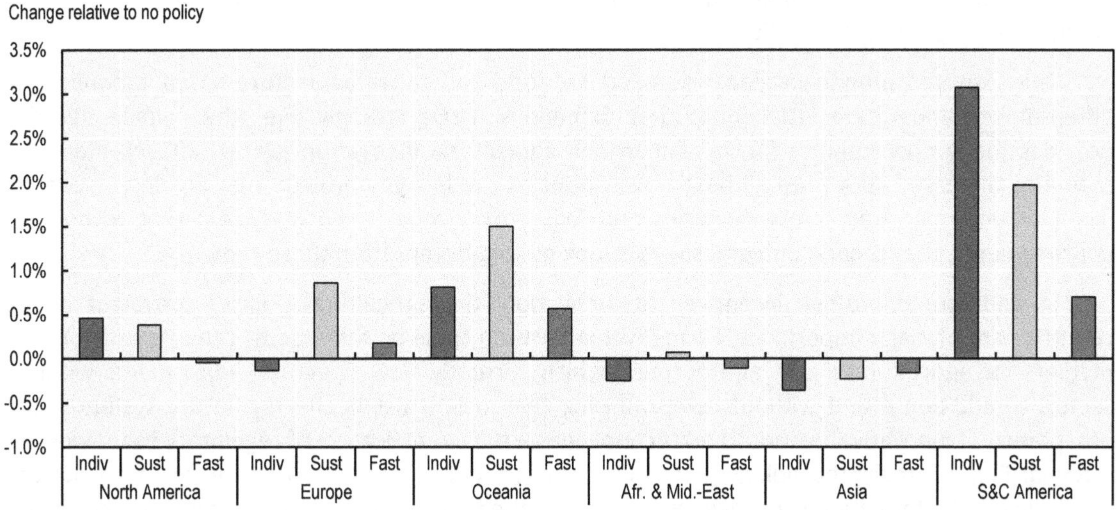

Change relative to no policy

Note: Trade cost reductions within and between the three large world regions are assumed to correspond to 5% and 15% of trade value relative to the Individual, Fossil Fuel-Driven Growth scenario, 10% and 10% relative to the Citizen-Driven, Sustainable Growth scenario, and 5% and 5% relative to the Fast, Globally-Driven scenario, respectively. The three world regions are defined to include the Americas; Europe, Africa and the Middle East; and Asia and Oceania. Changes shown are relative to the respective scenario without policy change.

Source: Results provided by the MAGNET model.

Sustainable productivity growth and climate resilience

Productivity growth and sustainable agriculture are mutually interdependent and will have to go hand-in-hand. Sufficient productivity growth is a precondition for the sustainability of agriculture in the long run. Conversely, the protection and efficient use of natural resources, such as land, water and soils, is necessary for achieving long-term productivity growth. The improvement of agricultural innovation systems and farming practices, and hence sustainable productivity growth, crucially depends on the involvement of a large range of stakeholders, including governments, non-governmental organisations, think-tanks, research institutes and labs, private industries, farmers and farm associations. This in turn requires corresponding institutions to enable the necessary collaboration. Farmers play a central role in developing and adopting innovation and will do so in response to related benefits.

Ensuring sustainable productivity growth will require a host of complementary activities. First and foremost, governments need to ensure a market and regulatory environment that is conducive to the development, distribution and application of appropriate methods and technologies. This environment also needs to enable private and public investors to make choices on which issues to focus in a world which is characterised by uncertainties. The availability of relevant information and undistorted market signals for decision makers, foresight activities, and networks involving all relevant stakeholders are therefore of key importance (Lopes, 2012). While such an environment will necessarily depend on specific countries' conditions, a number of key factors have been identified as drivers for productivity and sustainability (OECD, 2014b), including innovation, structural change and the use of natural resources.

These three drivers are in turn affected by a range of policies. Broadly speaking, these cover the stability of the economic system and institutions; the transparency and predictability of the environment, balancing the interests of investors and society and hence encouraging private investment; the provision of necessary public services; and targeted incentives for innovation, structural change and sustainable resource use. The private sector has a key role to play within the agricultural knowledge system. To fulfil this role, however, it depends on appropriate incentives to develop and diffuse information and technologies, including but not limited to a balanced system of intellectual property rights (OECD, 2012b).

The expected growth in global demand for food and other agriculture-based products – the different scenarios leave little doubt that demand will rise strongly over the coming decades – provides many opportunities for investments in agricultural innovation (OECD, 2013c). Indeed, the scenarios discussed above are all based on continued productivity growth and ongoing innovation – albeit at differing rates across scenarios and falling over time – and it is clear that without such improvements, the scenario outcomes would look quite different from those shown.

In addition to positive incentives to innovation, the agricultural policies prevalent in many countries are of major importance. Farm-level innovation could be fostered by removing distortions in markets for agricultural inputs and outputs, which currently slow structural adjustments within the sector. In addition – and without compromising the social trust in the regulatory system and the acceptance of innovative methods and technologies – the simplification of regulatory frameworks and safeguarding of their technology neutrality; the provision of infrastructure for transportation, marketing and information exchange; and agricultural education and extension systems are all key to ensure the required outcomes from the innovation system (OECD, 2013c).

The increased risks associated with climate change have led to greater focus on the improved resilience of agricultural production to climate-related shocks, such as the development of crop varieties resilient to heat, drought or excess precipitation and floods, and the improvement and expansion of crop irrigation systems. Such developments would have little impact on average market outcomes: results produced by the economic models suggest that the development of climate change-robust varieties[11] of wheat, maize and rice, the main staple food crops in large parts of the world, would increase the global output of these crops in 2050 by less than 2% in a high-climate change *Fast* world, and by much less than that in the *Sustainable* scenario, which assumes comparatively mild climate change. Improved irrigation systems, which enable the expansion of irrigated areas without additional water use, would have stronger impacts on high-irrigation crops such as rice.[12] Regardless of their impacts on average output, however, the improved climate-resilience which these developments would generate within the production system ensures that these are important elements of climate change adaptation strategies (see also Ignaciuk and Mason-D'Croz, 2014).

Sustainable productivity growth also needs to consider the reduction of GHG emissions and other pollutants per unit of agricultural output. Environmental degradation, or the emission of greenhouse gases beyond the damage-free stocking capacity of the atmosphere, can be viewed as specific forms of natural resource use and, more specifically, as common-pool resources (Cochran, 2012). As such, the concept of sustainable productivity growth itself needs to include these resources. In other words, working towards sustainable productivity growth through research and development, the deployment of new methods and technologies and public incentives requires an extended measurement of productivity to include not just priced production factors and inputs, but as much as possible the use and degradation of natural resources. Work on the development of an environmentally-adjusted multi-factor productivity measurement, which is underway at the OECD, is of key importance in this respect.

Finally, the reduction of food losses at the farm and storage levels is another important element of sustainable productivity growth. Where food waste along the supply chain is concerned, data is incomplete and incomparable across countries and time. Recent OECD work on food losses and waste in the People's Republic of China (hereafter "China") suggests, however, that losses at the level of post-harvest handling and storage represent a significant source of potential additional supplies (Liu, 2014). While losses on-farm and in storage in developing countries are often related to technical deficiencies, such as harvesting technologies, insect- and rodent infestations, mould, etc., losses in developed countries may more commonly be related to insufficient economic value in preserving and using available food products, partly because products do not meet the quality standards set by supermarket retailers (Bond et al., 2013).

Improved infrastructure

Improved and extended infrastructure is a key factor in the efficient connection of producers and consumers to markets, and in providing them with relevant resources. Physical infrastructure, including roads, railway networks and airport facilities, enable the connection of producers and consumers within both domestic and international markets. Increasingly, the availability of well-functioning ICT networks is another element of market development, including for food and agriculture.

The linkages between infrastructure development and growth in agricultural productivity and output have been well established (see, for example, Hanjra, Ferede and Gemechu Gutta, 2009, and sources cited in that paper). Improved transportation results in less costly domestic links between agricultural input suppliers, agricultural producers, food processors, and consumers, in addition to better connections to international markets for inputs and products. As a consequence, the efficiency of local and national markets is improved, allowing higher revenues for farmers but lower prices for final consumers.

The provision of physical infrastructure needs to carefully account for future changes in the environmental and economic context, as later adjustments of roads and other hard infrastructure are much more costly than the construction of new infrastructure. This is even more important in light of climate change, which may require the establishment of adjusted regional and international building standards for infrastructure and hence the close collaboration across disciplines, such as technical engineering and scientific research. Given the long-term investment nature of infrastructure projects, they require stable and multi-layer governance structures – generally involving local, regional, national and international levels – and long-term financing. Private investment appears to be of growing importance, but potential governance problems such as infrastructure monopolies need to be considered. At the same time, the need for multiple actors, multiple-layered governance structures, and multi-disciplinary approaches may represent key barriers to infrastructure development in less-developed regions.

Model results confirm that crop prices tend to increase with improved infrastructure. For the most part, however, these effects are found to be rather small. Global average producer prices for crops would increase by less than 0.3% in 2050, and only in South Africa, where infrastructure-related costs for agricultural products are comparatively high (GTAP, 2013), could the increase exceed 1%. Differences across scenarios are small, as the assumed cost reductions between primary and processed products are equal for the three scenarios analysed.

In turn, the model results also confirm that better infrastructure can have a price-lowering effect on processed food products. With up to 2% globally and up to 5% and more in the southern parts of Africa, these price reductions are found to potentially be markedly more pronounced than the price increases for primary products, suggesting that the majority of the benefits appear to be reaped by the downstream sector and consumers alike. Relative to the size of the price effects, the ranges across models are, however, quite large.

Other effects of improved infrastructure as found by the models are rather small, including generally positive impacts both on food security – calorie availability in 2050 would be up to 1% higher in Sub-Saharan Africa and South Asia – and farm incomes, which could increase by up to 4% in South Africa by 2050, slightly raising both labour use and wages. At the same time, however, agricultural land use in sensitive areas would also be higher, putting additional pressure on forests and other biodiverse land uses.

Other studies suggest that these results may underestimate the effects in specific areas. For instance, an analysis of the drivers for deforestation in the Congo Basin (Mosnier et al., 2014) suggests that better infrastructure would have the greatest benefits "for crops with good agronomic potential in remote areas" (p. 516). The infrastructure improvements would increase food demand for cassava, palm oil, sugar cane and sweet potatoes by between 6% and 15%, enhance exports of sugar cane and palm oil and reduce imports of other food products, thus improving the overall trade balance of the region. The study also supports the view, however, that Congo Basin forests would come under increasing pressure through expanded agricultural land use and through easier transportation of logs and hence better profitability of logging, with negative consequences for – in other words, rising levels of – forest-related GHG emissions. These results stress the importance of additional measures to enable the avoidance of negative trade-offs between agricultural and economic development, on the one hand, and damages to sensitive eco-systems on the other.

Improved and broadened risk management systems

As in other business sectors, agricultural production is subject to numerous risks which could originate in markets, e.g. unexpected changes in prices and volatile markets; climatic conditions, e.g. hail-related yield reductions; pests and diseases, e.g. livestock diseases lowering livestock productivity, killing animals or requiring the culling of herds; policies, e.g. closure of export markets due to SPS-related or geopolitical events; or others. Risks are also faced by consumers, generally in the form of unexpected fluctuations in food availability or volatile food prices and, as real threats, are largely limited to developing countries and poor households.

Some of these risks are more or less directly related to climatic conditions and could therefore be reinforced by climate change. Others, such as the occurrence of trans-boundary livestock diseases or the spreading of pests to other countries, could become more important as international trade in agricultural products increases. On the other hand, a well-functioning international trading system is capable of acting as a buffer against regional shocks, and hence of reducing the exposure of farmers and consumers within the affected region. The future of agricultural risks will therefore depend on the way agricultural systems and, more broadly, economies and policies, develop. The *Individual*, *Sustainable* and *Fast* scenarios are hence likely to each feature their own specific profile of risks:

- In an **Individual, Fossil Fuel-Driven Growth** world, the system is characterised by significant climate change-related and regionally-confined events, such as droughts, floods or storms. Given the focus on national and regional markets, trans-regional trade contributes relatively less to the spread of pests and diseases. The lack of international co-operation in strategies to combat these biological threats, however, raises pest and disease risks from within the regions. Political instability may add to local and regional risks. Moreover, as global trade in agricultural products is limited, countries are less buffered against shocks.
- In a **Citizen-Driven, Sustainable Growth** world, climate change would be less pronounced, and hence climate-related shocks are less frequent and less severe. Given the reduced focus on meat and other livestock products and hence less dense livestock production systems, animal diseases are less likely to spread within countries and regions, and lower international trade helps to reduce pressures from trans-boundary diseases. On the other hand, sudden episodes of large pest emergence could generate important regional shocks which are not well buffered by the international and trans-regional trading systems.
- In a **Fast, Globally-Driven Growth** world, international co-operation in the promotion of pest and disease control systems helps to lower regional biotic risks, but without additional sanitary and

phytosanitary border controls, emerging pests and diseases can spread across borders and regions in line with expanding trade volumes and could thus become systemic. Strong climate change adds abiotic risks which are related to extreme weather events. Systemic risks may also originate in very large multinationals in the food chain if some of these encounter significant economic difficulties. To some degree, the effects of such shocks are mitigated by the global exchange in technologies, information and products.

Agriculture requires a comprehensive and effective risk management system to address these specific risk profiles. This system should involve farmers and their associations, insurance and other financial industries, social security systems and governments.

Farm households need to take responsibility for business risks related to normal weather and market fluctuations, normal price volatility or limited biotic factors. The selection of specific production technologies may affect the exposure to individual risks or the ability of early detection and mitigation. On-farm strategies to reduce the economic impact of specific events may include, among others, various diversification measures, including longer crop rotations, crop-livestock combinations etc. The farm-household may add to that diversification by creating additional revenues. Savings can help to balance temporary revenue declines, as can adjustments in consumption or the take-up of additional off-farm work or borrowing from neighbours, the larger family or the community (OECD, 2009).

Farm associations may, for instance, play an important role in creating transparency regarding risk management options; in helping to pool risks and hence to reduce individual farmers' exposure; and in collecting and providing data required for other risk management levels.[13]

A range of risk management options related both to market risks, such as volatile prices, and to biotic or abiotic shocks, are available within the market. These include, among others, risk management training for farmers, insurance, financial activities such as futures and options, banking systems allowing saving and borrowing, various forms of vertical integration, the diversification of marketing activities and different contracting forms.

Finally, governments at different levels need to ensure institutional and market environments that enable risk reduction and mitigation. This may include, among other things, a stable and conducive macroeconomic framework; the generation of and access to relevant information and data; disaster prevention measures, including the protection against both biotic and abiotic risks; reliable tax and social security systems, etc. In the case of catastrophic events which go beyond the buffering capacity of the private market, governments need to provide disaster relief and similar assistance (OECD, 2009). This latter type of intervention should, however, be limited to events with which the agricultural and insurance system is unable to cope, such as large-scale floods or droughts, earthquakes etc. Public intervention in these cases should also be subject to well-defined damage thresholds, as well as transparent protocols, in order to avoid crowding out market-based risk management mechanisms or the over-specialisation or under-insurance of farm households.

From broad strategies towards their implementation

How, then, can these and related broad strategies be translated into actionable steps to ensure and accelerate their implementation? A range of players need to be involved, and action is required both individually and in collaboration. The list of players goes beyond the types of stakeholders which were directly involved in the development and analysis of the OECD scenarios, and includes, among others, the private industry – the farming sector, as well as up- and downstream industries, including the retail sector; civil society and related NGOs; and a range of international organisations.

Cross-cutting themes

A number of cross-cutting themes have been identified which affect the implementation of various strategies. These include the availability of information, the understanding and development of attitudes and lifestyles, continued work on international guidelines and standards, the importance of subsidiarity, and the fundamental role of education.

The **availability of information** is of prime importance, not only for the development and implementation of policies and investment decisions, but for the identification of policy and investment requirements as well as for the assessment of their impacts. Developing countries, however, often lack up-to-date and sufficiently detailed market data, and surveillance and early-warning systems, such as those for livestock diseases, are not readily available. Both developing and developed countries also face challenges in obtaining data on consumer food choices. Some information may already be available to the industry – e.g. retailers who collect purchase data through loyalty cards and other means – and finding means to make use of such information without compromising privacy and business interests will be important steps forward. The advent of "big data" within the agriculture and food sectors could therefore open new and promising opportunities, including for service providers. At the same time, there are some policy challenges, such as those related to data protection and data property rights and to the control of air space when data acquisition takes place via unmanned air vehicles.

Attitudes and lifestyles may represent both barriers to *and* drivers of change. Consumers may distrust certain technologies, and individuals may undervalue the notification of livestock diseases. There is a strong need for the better showcasing of the benefits of innovation while improving citizens' trust by encouraging a frank and open exchange on potential risks, based on the scientific evidence available, and considering the different approaches which exist across countries with respect to the precautionary principle. This also includes a need for continued efforts to maintain or enhance scientific standards, including those on transparency, notably in the event of conflicting scientific results. Similar showcasing is required of the benefits of notifying livestock diseases as well as other issues. On the other hand, the fostering of responsible business conduct (see, for example, OECD, 2011b) and socially responsible investments is an important driver of change at both domestic and international levels. Consumer demand for new and high-quality food products or non-market goods may also create additional incentives for innovation. At the same time, it should be noted that lifestyles are constantly developing, and that numerous factors can influence these.

A number of public and private organisations at national and international levels are already developing **international guidelines and standards** in the areas of food regulation and trans-boundary livestock diseases, amongst others. There is however a need for better identification of best practices for standard-setting. In addition, international co-operation should not be limited to regulations and standards per se, but should increasingly focus on related processes such as data generation, risk assessment and conformity assessment procedures. Better co-ordination is also required to help small and medium-sized enterprises in developing countries in particular, which may face difficulties in complying with increasingly complex regulations in domestic and foreign markets.

In order to properly respond to challenges in food and agriculture, **subsidiarity** remains a key principle across policy areas. Subsidiarity entails a clear definition of responsibilities across public and private players, for instance in the area of risk management systems. It also concerns the regional level of action which strongly depends on the type of problem at hand. For instance, the environmental performance of agricultural production has local, regional and global dimensions, and responses in terms of policies, technological or method developments need to be found at the corresponding levels.

Finally, almost all areas discussed in this chapter heavily depend on investments in **education**, both of farmers and of the general public. This touches on issues such as the management of livestock diseases and other risks of farming, the application of innovative production methods, and the development of more sustainable diet and consumption habits. Education has an even more fundamental role in the development of societies and economies within developing countries in particular. Differences across the three scenarios demonstrate that population growth and economic development are among the most relevant drivers for the evolution of agricultural markets in developing countries. Both of these are strongly influenced by better education.

Who needs to be involved?

Key roles were identified for **governments** at different levels. These include, among others, the co-ordination of policies on food security and sustainability, regulation and economic tools to correct market failures such as the lack of integration of costs related to environmental externalities, the funding and orientation of research, technological transfer and adoption, and the participation in international science and research co-operation. Governments also need to provide support to innovative experiments and outreach. There is a need for strengthened links between policy and research, where policy needs drive research activities in order to be properly informed by the research outcomes. Governments are actively involved in international standard-setting where improved co-operation is required. Continued close collaboration is also needed to limit climate change, most immediately in the context of the Conference of the Parties to the UNFCCC, and to address other global environmental and food security challenges. Governments also need to become more transparent and coherent with respect to their long-term strategies, including on food and agriculture. Political choices are based on the dichotomy between societal preferences and the evidence-base. Bringing the two together requires the availability and filtering of information from different channels.

Research institutes are required to focus on improving the quality of their research and its applicability for policy advice. For policy makers, the relative uncertainties of scientific results, such as those from quantitative modelling, often make the use of these results quite difficult.

The **OECD** and its **Secretariat** are called upon to tailor its policy advice to individual countries and regions, taking their level of development and other characteristics into account. It needs to provide bold advice, such as on innovation policies. There is also an increasing need to bridge existing gaps between short-term and long-term policy advice, as well as between general policy advice and its practical implementation. Given its multi-sector, multi-country coverage, the work by the OECD Secretariat is of importance to governments, and many of its ongoing activities are seen as necessary to prepare for future challenges facing food and agriculture. These activities include both the continued provision of market and policy information and work on specific issues, such as that on agricultural innovation systems, private standards and public regulations in food and agriculture, and others. Depending on the topic, continued collaboration with other International Organisations and enhanced dialogue with different stakeholders is increasingly important.

The **private sector** has a number of important responsibilities. The food and agricultural sectors have a key role to play in driving productivity growth and sustainability within the framework set by public policies. This includes areas such as research and development and the provision and sharing of data. Furthermore, the industry can play an important role in consumer information, making the food industry a key partner for governments.

Within the private sector, the **farming community** needs to take responsibility in various areas, including risk management, innovation and quality management. Farmers will need to adapt to an environment that changes in numerous aspects related to climatic, economic and political conditions. Both basic and continued education therefore plays an important role within the agricultural sector.

Finally, a wide range of other **existing structures, processes and forums** were identified that do relevant work related to the long-term challenges facing food and agriculture. These include the International Standard-Setting Bodies, International Organisations (e.g. FAO, UNEP, WTO, the World Bank), regional and international agricultural research groups (e.g. the Consultative Group on International Agricultural Research and the Global Research Alliance), regional economic communities in different parts of the world, and several international private initiatives and partnerships. Importantly, a number of other food-related foresight activities could provide useful cross-fertilisation with the OECD work related to long-term developments in food and agriculture.

The challenge of seizing the opportunities

Although the future of food and agriculture remains unpredictable, the scenarios developed and analysed above highlight a number of challenges. For the most part, these are already observable today, but their future will unfold depending on a large number of factors and drivers. The scenarios enable understanding of the linkages between drivers and challenges, as well as between challenges, even if none of the scenarios is more likely to be true than the others, and indeed many more scenarios could have been imagined and discussed.

Analysis of the scenarios also revealed a number of *opportunities* for action by policy makers, industry, civil society and citizens to alter the outcomes of food and agriculture systems over the coming decades. In many cases, suggested strategies are robust strategies, which have positive effects on various challenges and across scenarios, with no – or only limited – negative side-effects, even if the magnitude of the benefits may depend on regional, climatic, economic or other conditions. Among these robust strategies are measures to boost sustainable productivity growth, including research and development activities, a conducive institutional framework and international exchange of ideas and technologies. The mainstreaming of more sustainable consumption patterns and lifestyles could, similar to productivity growth, free up scarce resources by reducing the rapidly increasing demand for agricultural and food products.

Other strategies entail more of a trade-off, however. The improvement of rural and regional infrastructure in developing countries, for example, is a key factor in their development, helping to link remote production or consumption centres to national and international markets and to stimulate important economic development, both within agriculture and in other sectors. At the same time, such infrastructure may have direct and indirect environmental costs, including greater incentives for logging and land use change. Similarly, while the expansion of international trade in food and agriculture helps to improve the efficiency of global resource use, it may equally foster the risk of trans-boundary livestock diseases, pests or invasive species; increase the need for adapted food safety systems; and generate environmental costs due to extended transportation activities. In addition, risks related to global commons may be exacerbated if countries' engagement and commitment on global sustainability differ and if international management mechanisms lag behind trade opening. In virtually all scenarios and policy strategies, farmers will need to adjust, and structural change will continue to affect the sectorial landscape.

How, then, can the different strategies be made more operational, and how can potential trade-offs and negative side-effects be minimised? In addition to other efforts, work undertaken by the OECD points to a number of short- to medium-term decisions which can potentially improve the outcomes of the agriculture and food system. Some of these processes are either ongoing or are on the agenda of international negotiations.

In many areas, for example, existing policies continue to present obstacles to the achievement of desired outcomes in the food and agriculture systems. Such policies can be specific to the agricultural sector, such as measures hampering the required structural change, agricultural trade or important innovation and its widespread application; or relevant for other sectors, including distortive support, e.g. for the use of fossil energy. Policies such as these often have specific objectives, e.g. rural development or poverty reduction, which can be pursued more efficiently with more targeted measures. Other policies, such as the promotion of specific non-food uses of biomass, both of agricultural and other origin, should be reviewed for their contribution to the stated objectives and in light of the existing pressures on natural resources.

Other policy adjustments are underway on the international agenda. International and regional efforts are currently focused on improving the rules in international trade. Increasing the fluidity of trade links without compromising legitimate domestic objectives for food safety, environmental protection and other areas is important to enable the achievement of the full benefits of comparative advantages. Co-operation on environmental challenges, most prominently in the area of greenhouse gas emissions and climate change, could result in major improvements in the consideration of common-pool resources such as the atmosphere and its capacity to absorb pollutants.

Some areas require close collaboration between public and private players. For instance, the OECD (2012b) highlights a number of areas within the agricultural knowledge and innovation system where the public sector and the private industry each have their specific roles, but where partnerships between the two can generate additional synergies. Given increasingly tight public budgets, funding for research and development will need private engagement, by means of levies on agricultural revenues, for example. Furthermore, the development of new methods and technologies needs to be combined with their broad dissemination and deployment: farmers and the private sector need to be involved in both development and implementation, including the showcasing of innovative approaches and their benefits.

Maintaining the ability to adjust

Given the lack of predictability surrounding future challenges and the likelihood of "unknown unknowns" which may create disruptions or unforeseen changes in pathways, strategies at both public and private levels need to remain sufficiently flexible to adjust to new evidence. For a number of uncertainties identified through this and other work, new knowledge is likely to alter both the prospects and the expectations surrounding these. For instance, a key factor driving the differences in the results across economic models is the assumption on how easily or costly additional land can be brought into agricultural production or switched between different agricultural uses. More interdisciplinary work, involving scientists, economists and others is required in order to shed more light on this region-specific question, and hopefully better and more conclusive information on this will become available in the coming years. Other examples are the development of new technologies or business models, or changing habits related to food consumption. In addition to these fundamental drivers, sudden and unforeseen events of natural or human origin may disrupt developments and it is important that these are also considered (Box 3.1).

As a consequence, the scenarios developed and used at the OECD are key to challenging views and assumptions – while also being challenged themselves. Policy strategies and steps towards their implementation need to be broad and bold, yet at the same time, governments must avoid being locked into rigid strategies which prevent them from responding to new information or trends. The same naturally holds for private initiatives, although, given its greater experience with scenario approaches, the private sector is likely to be better prepared for a changing environment.

Box 3.1. A large (potentially very large) range of disrupting events not explicitly covered by this study

In the development and discussion of the scenarios, many other factors and possible events could have been considered. In particular, these include sudden and dramatic breaks in developments and so-called "black swan" events: unknowns for which the nature, location, timing, magnitude and impacts cannot be properly assessed, often because they have not occurred in documented history or, if they have, the context in which they might impact societies has substantially changed. Such events may create major disruptions of a temporary (if extended) nature, or generate breaks in existing trends and hence affect future pathways in general. A number of such events can be imagined, and are touched upon occasionally by media or academia. Prominently among these are natural disasters of global dimensions and major shifts in world economic conditions. Representative of many other possible events, one could think of major volcano eruptions.

Major volcano eruptions may have significant local and regional implications in terms of the direct damage incurred by pyroclastic flows and the subsequent fall of volcanic ash. In addition, tsunamis may have disastrous impacts on coastal areas which are potentially very distant from the eruption itself. More indirectly, the longer-term consequences of large eruptions may include disruptions in regional or global air traffic and, related to this, supply chains, potentially hurting economies far more strongly than the original damage. As shown by the eruption of the Eyjafjallajokull in Iceland 2010, which was comparatively small in a longer-term context, losses to the aviation industry can quickly amount to billions of dollars, with indirect economic damages much larger than this, which can spread to much larger regions, if not globally. Longer-term still, the sulphur emitted into the atmosphere may reflect significant proportions of the incoming solar radiation, potentially leading to an overall cooling of the planet's surface temperatures, with potentially strong implications for regional and global agricultural production and supply. The eruption of the Tambora in Indonesia in 1815, the most powerful eruption in modern history, resulted in a fall in average global summer temperatures by about 1°C the following year. Regional temperature deviations were even larger. In particular, land temperatures dropped about twice as much, and rainfall declined by up to 4% in 1816. Significant food shortages in different parts of the world were among the consequences (The Economist, 2015).

Another example of developments not well captured by the scenarios in this work is a potentially much larger, either temporary or permanent, change in energy markets. For instance, if the current period of low oil prices, followed by other fossil fuels, is extended for a longer period of time, some analysts believe that major investments in oil, gas and coal extraction may be put on hold. This would reinforce trends driven by increasing emission reduction targets and improved fuel efficiencies. It is feared that the lack of investment today will risk dramatically increasing energy prices over the medium-term (Randall, 2014).

Other events with potentially global implications may include the spread of terrorism beyond limited regional scales, failure of major economies and global epidemics.

Concluding observations

Main findings for food and agriculture

- The scenarios discussed in this report suggest that the era of falling real **agricultural prices** may have come to an end. Nevertheless, while some studies on the future of agriculture indicate that global markets may be under continued and significant stress, with significantly rising food prices, the outcomes of the OECD scenarios suggest that future price increases should remain more limited. This result is, however, an outcome of the specifics of both the three scenarios and of their quantification and therefore not a projection that would contradict other findings. Price paths differ across the three scenarios and the four models used, and neither these scenarios nor the four models selected should be seen as representative for other scenarios and models.

- The end of significantly falling real agricultural prices does not necessarily imply a dramatic deterioration of the global **food security** situation. Instead, some of the drivers behind improved food security, including notably economic growth and the development of larger middle-classes in emerging and developing economies, could contribute to lifting prices above their long-term historical trend. Nevertheless, the results of the scenario analysis undertaken for this study reveal large variations between scenarios in the degree and speed of progress towards food security. Progress to be made in an *Individual* scenario, which can be seen as a business-as-usual scenario with little focus on sustainability or international co-operation, would be much too limited. International co-operation and sustainable productivity growth, as well as reductions in food losses and food waste, are crucial to resolve food insecurity worldwide. These should be accompanied by improved risk management systems, dealing with volatile markets and prices, and systems to reduce transitory food insecurity, in order to address the different instabilities inherent within the three scenarios.

- Rising per capita incomes also contribute to more variable and elaborate **diets**, particularly in Africa and Asia, where the consumption of livestock products and higher-value crop products increases at the expense of staple crops such as roots and food grains. This is most pronounced in a *Fast* world, with highest income growth rates, and should improve the nutritional status and health of food consumers beyond the increase in energy availability. At the same time, risks related to food over-consumption and the rising consumption of meat, sugar and fats may increase health risks in an increasing number of countries, including in the developing world, if adjustments to diets and lifestyles are not made.

- For farmers around the world, an end to falling agricultural prices would create substantial opportunities and, in a context of further productivity growth, raise **farm incomes**. This is particularly the case in land-abundant regions, but also in Asia, where productivity and farm incomes lag behind other regions. Growth potential in most industrialised regions is, in contrast, more limited. In addition, a major shift towards more sustainable lifestyles would require significant adjustments in the farming sector.

- Despite these comparably positive prospects, **structural change** within the agricultural sector will continue to play a major role in ensuring the remaining farms' economic sustainability. Relative to the overall economy, the agricultural share in both GDP and in employment are bound to shrink further, with labour mostly moving towards expanding service and non-food manufacturing sectors. This process is most pronounced in the *Fast* and *Sustainable* scenarios, and is both a result and a driver of agricultural productivity. At the same time, the viability and well-being of rural areas is of key importance for governments in all countries.

- With further expansion of agricultural land use and the growing use of farm inputs, in developing and emerging economies in particular, the *Individual* and *Fast* scenarios suggest serious threats to sensitive **habitats and ecosystems**, with potentially significant losses in biodiversity. Even in the *Sustainable* scenario, which features substantially reduced demand for meat and other livestock products, forests in Sub-Saharan Africa and Latin America would continue to decline without dedicated protective action, albeit at lower rates than in the two other scenarios. Similar findings are made with regard to agricultural **greenhouse gas emissions and other pollutants**, which could continue to increase in both the *Individual* and *Fast* scenarios, even if more slowly than agricultural output and comparatively less in a *Sustainable* world.

- While other drivers appear to be of greater importance to the global development of agricultural and food markets and related outcomes, **climate change** may pose significant risks at the regional and local levels and increase the variability of weather and hence productivity and prices. Without greater efforts to combat climate change and to mitigate its negative effects, stronger economic growth – key driver to improving the fate of billions of impoverished people – will likely increase greenhouse gas emissions and hence negatively affect the productive capacity of the agricultural sector.

- **Trans-boundary livestock diseases** are found to remain a threat to global agriculture, particularly in the meat-rich *Individual* and *Fast* scenarios. This also holds for threats to food safety, given the high use of farm inputs and, notably within the latter of these two scenarios, long and multinational food chains. Food companies will increasingly be responsible for tracing food ingredients and ensuring safe food for consumers. Risks related to food safety and trans-boundary diseases may be somewhat weaker in a *Sustainable* world, given the reduced livestock production, lower use of farm input and shorter and more localised food supply chains. Without international co-operation on food regulation and controls, however, these risks remain important.

Opportunities to secure better outcomes

- **Focus on sustainable productivity growth is required to secure the future of the food and agriculture system.** Sustainable development and progress in agricultural productivity represent the two sides of the same coin. Governments should review their existing policies and reconsider measures that effectively create barriers to sustainable productivity growth and related adjustments. Such policies include distortive measures that prevent or slow down improvements in the allocation of production factors across regions, sectors and firms. A telling example is the support for the use of fossil energy or other energy-intensive inputs in agricultural production. Sustainable productivity growth also requires a well-functioning agricultural innovation system, involving both public and private actors. Furthermore, while structural change is not an end in itself, it has been shown to be a key driver of productivity growth. Finally, an improved measurement of sustainable productivity growth needs to account for the use of natural resources, including common pool resources such as fresh water and the emission of GHGs and other pollutants. The development of related indicators, including in the context of the OECD work on Green Growth, such as the *Environmentally Adjusted Multifactor Productivity*, is of key importance for this.
- **Opportunities for improving the outcomes for food and agriculture are not limited to changes in agricultural policies**. Instead, a variety of policy areas will need to contribute to more robust strategies, including in the area of up- and downstream industries as well as the general economy, education, health, environment, climate-proof infrastructure and others. An increased focus on policy coherence across these policy fields is therefore indispensable, highlighting the multi-disciplinary nature of the challenges at hand.
- **Public authorities' actions increasingly need to be complemented by private involvement**. While governments should play a key role by providing the required institutional and regulatory environment, resolving market failures and investing in public goods and services, private companies, farmers, the research community, consumers and the civil society are also important players. Responsible business conduct and socially responsible investments are key elements at national and international levels. A number of strategic areas involve both public and private entities, such as research, development and extension, the generation and dissemination of data, the provision of relevant information to consumers to enable informed and responsible decisions, and the management of risks related to farming. Farmers, for example, need to develop, test and adopt new methods, technologies and forms of horizontal and vertical integration, which are important elements in sustainable productivity growth, while food processors and retailers should help to ensure effective communications within the food chain around supply capacity and market demands. Consumers, for their part, can play a role via their purchasing decisions, while citizens can influence political processes. Constructive, co-ordinated action between all of these actors will, however, require improved systems of co-operation and communication across stakeholders.
- **Agricultural risk management systems should be improved and their use extended**. Risk management systems, including insurance and banking systems and adapted and reliable tax and social security systems, will become increasingly critical for the management of volatile markets resulting from a multitude of weather, policy or technological shocks. Farm households, farm

associations, insurers, other financial industries and governments all have central roles to play in their improvement and dissemination.

- **National and regional variations in lifestyles and attitudes should be taken into account within strategies to accelerate movement towards more sustainable lifestyles and consumption trends.** Lifestyles and mentalities can create significant barriers to change, e.g. consumer reluctance to accept new technologies or products. They may however also represent a *driver* to change, as evident in the greater emphasis which is being placed by increasing segments of – mainly industrialised countries' – populations on the quality and sustainable production process of the food that they consume. Actions aimed at accelerating this shift to more sustainable lifestyles should involve all stakeholders, and should be tailored to national and regional lifestyles and mindsets.

- **International cooperation in various areas can – and *should* – be further improved**, including with regard to global commons such as the climate and sustainability, international trade, regulatory coherence and the well-functioning of global markets, R&D and international spill-overs of technological developments, and others. International research efforts not only need to focus on sustainable productivity growth, but also on improving our understanding of key linkages between physical (e.g. atmospheric GHG concentrations and climate change), biological (e.g. crop and livestock productivity in different agro-climatic conditions) and behavioural variables (e.g. consumers' long-term response to large changes in income). Although growth-focused collaboration at the international level can help progress in many areas, this needs to be complemented by collaboration in the sustainability and social areas in particular.

- **Further analysis of policies which impact these issues is needed.** Of continued relevance are ongoing work on agricultural policies, their measurement and evaluation, including on their role in promoting or hampering adjustments within the sector; on policies affecting sustainable productivity growth, including the development and refinement of the innovation framework and the measurement of sustainable productivity in the context of Green Growth; on the benefits of and measures towards more open trade, including international regulatory co-operation, and others.

- Finally, **the scenarios discussed in this report should continue to be enriched, refined and challenged**, both within the OECD and elsewhere, with the involvement of all relevant stakeholders. Where possible, they need to be "regionalised" or even "nationalised" to enable more tailored policy advice. The reasons for this are twofold: first, the majority of the priority challenges facing agriculture will develop differently across regions and time, due to climatic, geopolitical or other disruptions. There is a need for more detailed analysis of policy options which take the economic, social, political and other realities in different countries into account. Secondly, questions related to the heterogeneity which exists within societies and farm sectors, the structure of value chains, market volatility and shocks to food and agriculture systems require further work, and many of these can be better explored within regionally limited but more detailed settings.

Notes

1. The general strategy areas have been identified in the lead up to and during the first OECD Workshop on Long-Term Scenarios for Food and Agriculture, Paris, 2013. A more detailed discussion of these strategies took place at the second OECD Workshop on Long-Term Scenarios for Food and Agriculture, Paris, 2014.

2. Second OECD Workshop on Long-Term Scenarios for Food and Agriculture, Paris, 2014.

3. Recent OECD analysis shows that despite significant media and public attention, the precise scale and pattern of food waste along the food supply chain remains poorly understood. While data for household food losses are relatively reliable, coverage of other areas of the supply chain remains insufficient (Bagherzadeh, Inamura and Jeong, 2014). Case study evidence from Japan and the United Kingdom suggests that the reduction of food losses and waste has been a major policy objective in these two countries for a number of years. In both countries, food waste within the food industry has been reduced, yet while household food waste declined by 15% in the United Kingdom, no change in consumer food waste could be identified for Japan. These findings suggest that despite the significant potential which exists, the reduction of waste at the household level in particular remains a challenging policy task (Parry, Bleazard and Okawa, 2015).

4. See: www.bbc.com/future/story/20140603-are-maggots-the-future-of-food.

5. See: www.forbes.com/sites/amywestervelt/2012/05/04/forget-fuel-algae-could-help-feed-the-world.

6. See: www.bbc.com/news/science-environment-23576143.

7. See: www.arc.agric.za/arc-vopi/Pages/Crop%20Science/Hydroponic-Vegetable-Production.aspx.

8. See: www.soylent.me.

9. Details on the set-up of the different policy experiments can be found in Annex C.

10. As outlined in further detail below, coherence should normally be considered both across countries and regions, as a means to help international trade, and across policy objectives to improve policy effectiveness and efficiency. This section focuses on improved coherence across countries and regions.

11. Simulations assume that one-third of the (scenario-, region- and crop-specific) climate-induced yield damage can be avoided.

12. This experiment assumes a 20% improvement in water use efficiency and the re-utilisation of the saved water by expanded irrigation areas. See Annex 1.A2 for a description of the different policy experiments.

13. Second OECD Workshop on Long-Term Scenarios for Food and Agriculture, Paris, 2014.

References

Bagherzadeh, M., M. Inamura and H. Jeong (2014), "Food Waste Along the Food Chain", *OECD Food, Agriculture and Fisheries Papers*, No. 71, OECD Publishing, Paris, http://dx.doi.org/10.1787/5jxrcmftzj36-en.

Baldos, U.L.C. and T. W. Hertel (2015), "The role of international trade in managing food security risks from climate change", *Food Security,* Vol. 7/2, pp. 275-290, Springer, Netherlands, http://link.springer.com/article/10.1007/s12571-015-0435-z.

Bond, M. et al. (2013), *Food Waste within Global Food Systems*, Global Food Security Programme, www.foodsecurity.ac.uk/assets/pdfs/food-waste-report.pdf.

Brooks, J. and A. Matthews (2015), "Trade Dimensions of Food Security", *OECD Food, Agriculture and Fisheries Papers*, No. 77, OECD Publishing, Paris, http://dx.doi.org/10.1787/5js65xn790nv-en.

Cochran, I. (2012), "On the Commons and Climate Change: Collective Action and GHG Mitigation", *CDC Climate Research Working Paper*, No. 2012-13, France, www.cdcclimat.com/IMG/pdf/12-07_cdc_climat_r_wp_12-13_commons_and_climate_change-2.pdf.

Foresight (2010), *Workshop Report: W4 Expert Forum on the Reduction of Food Waste*, The Government Office for Science, London, http://s3.amazonaws.com/zanran_storage/www.bis.gov.uk/ContentPages/2374836301.pdf.

GTAP (2013), *GTAP Version 8.1* (database), published February 2013, www.gtap.agecon.purdue.edu/databases/v8/default.asp (accessed July 2014).

Hanjra, M.A., T. Ferede and D.G. Gutta, (2009), "Reducing poverty in Sub-Saharan Africa through investments in water and other priorities", *Agricultural Water Management*, Vol. 96/7, pp. 1062–1070, Elsevier, http://dx.doi.org/10.1016/j.agwat.2009.03.001.

Ignaciuk, A. and D. Mason-D'Croz, (2014), "Modelling Adaptation to Climate Change in Agriculture", *OECD Food, Agriculture and Fisheries Papers*, No. 70, OECD Publishing, Paris, http://dx.doi.org/10.1787/5jxrclljnbxq-en.

Liu, G. (2014), "Food Losses and Food Waste in China: A First Estimate", *OECD Food, Agriculture and Fisheries Papers*, No. 66, OECD Publishing, Paris, http://dx.doi.org/10.1787/5jz5sq5173lq-en.

Lopes, M. (2012), "The Brazilian Agricultural Research for Development (ARD) System", in OECD, *Improving Agricultural Knowledge and Innovation Systems: OECD Conference Proceedings*, OECD Publishing, Paris, http://dx.doi.org/10.1787/9789264167445-27-en.

Moomaw, W. et al. (2012), "The Critical Role of Global Food Consumption Patterns in Achieving Sustainable Food Systems and Food for All: A UNEP Discussion Paper", United Nations Environment Programme, Division of Technology, Industry and Economics, Paris, http://fletcher.tufts.edu/CIERP/~/media/Fletcher/Microsites/CIERP/Publications/2012/UNEP%20Global%20Food%20Consumption.pdf.

Mosnier, A. et al. (2014), "Modeling impact of development trajectories and a global agreement on reducing emissions from deforestation on Congo Basin forests by 2030", *Environmental Resource*

Economics, Vol. 57/4, pp. 505-525, Springer, Netherlands, http://dx.doi.org/10.1007/s10640-012-9618-7.

OECD (2014a), *OECD Economic Outlook,* Issue 2/96, November 2014, OECD Publishing, Paris, http://dx.doi.org/10.1787/eco_outlook-v2014-2-en.

OECD (2014b), *Analysing Policies to Improve Agricultural Productivity Growth, Sustainably: Draft Framework*, OECD Publishing, Paris, www.oecd.org/tad/agricultural-policies/Analysing-policies-improve-agricultural-productivity-growth-sustainably-december-2014.pdf.

OECD (2012a), *OECD Environmental Outlook to 2050: The Consequences of Inaction*, OECD Publishing, Paris, http://dx.doi.org/10.1787/9789264122246-en.

OECD (2012b), *Improving Agricultural Knowledge and Innovation Systems: OECD Conference Proceedings*, OECD Publishing, Paris, http://dx.doi.org/10.1787/9789264167445-en.

OECD (2012c), *Agricultural Innovation Systems: A Framework for Analysing the Role of the Government*, OECD Publishing, Paris, http://dx.doi.org/10.1787/9789264200593-en.

OECD (2011a), *The Impact of Trade Liberalisation on Jobs and Growth: Technical Note, OECD Trade Policy Papers, No. 107*, OECD Publishing, Paris, http://dx.doi.org/10.1787/5kgj4jfj1nq2-en.

OECD (2011b), *OECD Guidelines for Multinational Enterprises: Responsible Business Conduct Matters*, OECD Publishing, Paris, https://mneguidelines.oecd.org/MNEguidelines_RBCmatters.pdf.

OECD (2009), *Managing Risk in Agriculture: A Holistic Approach*, OECD Publishing, Paris, http://dx.doi.org/10.1787/9789264075313-en.

Parry, A., P. Bleazard, P. and K. Okawa (2015), *Preventing Food Waste: Case Studies of Japan and the United Kingdom*, OECD Food, Agriculture and Fisheries Papers, No. 76, OECD Publishing, Paris. http://dx.doi.org/10.1787/5js4w29cf0f7-en.

Randal, T. (2014), "Bankers see $1 trillion of zombie investments stranded in the oil fields", *Bloomberg Business*, 18 December 2014, www.bloomberg.com/news/articles/2014-12-18/bankers-see-1-trillion-of-investments-stranded-in-the-oil-fields#news/articles.

The Economist (2015), "After Tambora", *The Economist*, 11 April 2015, www.economist.com/news/briefing/21647958-two-hundred-years-ago-most-powerful-eruption-modern-history-made-itself-felt-around.

UNRISD (2011), *Emerging Governance in the Transition to a Green Economy: A Case Study of Public Sector Food Procurement in Brazil*, United Nations Research Institute for Social Development, Geneva, www.unrisd.org/80256B3C005BE6B5/search/5FE39DD0008CDBBDC125793B0044E218?OpenDocument.

ANNEXES

Annex A

Models used for the quantification of scenarios and policy experiments

To quantify key elements of the different scenarios and simulate some of the strategy options for analysing their potential effects on the outcomes for food and agriculture systems, four global economic models have been used, including two computable general-equilibrium (CGE) models and two partial-equilibrium (PE) models:

ENVISAGE: The Environmental Impact and Sustainability Applied General Equilibrium (ENVISAGE) model is a descendent of models developed in the 1980s by Stanford University, the Université Libre de Bruxelles and the OECD. It began at the World Bank in 2007 as a re-coded version of the World Bank's LINKAGE model. It is designed specifically to analyse climate change issues and thus incorporates a detailed energy sector; a climate module, that makes integrated assessment an option; and climate change impact feedbacks. The current version relies on the GTAP v.8 database with the 2007 base year and allows flexible aggregation from GTAP's 57 commodities, of which 22 are agricultural and food products. More details on ENVISAGE can be found in van der Mensbrugghe (2010).

GLOBIOM: The Global Biosphere Management Model (GLOBIOM) has been developed and used by the International Institute for Applied Systems Analysis (IIASA) since the late 2000s. The partial-equilibrium model represents various land use-based activities, including agriculture, forestry and bioenergy sectors. The model is built following a bottom-up setting based on detailed grid-cell information, providing the biophysical and technical cost information. This detailed structure allows a rich set of environmental parameters to be taken into account. Its spatial equilibrium modelling approach represents bilateral trade based on cost competitiveness. The model was initially developed for the integrated assessment of climate change mitigation policies in land-based sectors, including biofuels, and is also increasingly being implemented for agricultural and timber markets foresight, and economic impact analysis of climate change and adaptation. More details on GLOBIOM can be found in Havlík et al. (2011, 2014).

IMPACT: From its beginnings in the early 1990s, the International Model for Policy Analysis of Agricultural Commodities and Trade (IMPACT), developed by the International Food Policy Research Institute (IFPRI), focused on simulating the linkages between the production of over 50 agricultural commodities and food demand and security at national level in the context of scenarios of future change. For this analysis, production takes place in some 320 food production units (based on river basin) and with separate analysis for irrigated and rain-fed cultivation. Similar to the majority of other partial equilibrium models, the net-trade approach in IMPACT abstracts from bilateral trade flows or simultaneous imports and exports and, apart from policy-induced price wedges and marketing margins, assumes full price transmission across markets. More details on IMPACT can be found in Rosegrant et al. (2012).

MAGNET: The Modular Applied GeNeral Equilibrium Tool (MAGNET) of LEI, part of Wageningen-UR, has specifically focused on agriculture since the mid-nineties. Agricultural policies, trade policies, heterogeneous factor markets and technological change (GMOs, knowledge spill-overs) were focus areas. Growing out of a long-run co-operation with the biophysical climate change impact assessment model IMAGE of the Dutch environment agency, PBL (Eickhout et al. 2009), the focus shifted to the long-run analysis, including issues such as and land use and endogenous yield effects. More recently the model has been extended to include first-generation biofuels, fertilisers and the implementation of REDD policies. Despite its complexity, the model is flexible in aggregation across regions and commodities. MAGNET uses the GTAP v.8 database with a 2007 base year, with additional updated base years 2004 and 2007. More details on MAGNET can be found in Woltjer and Kuiper (2014).

References for Annex A

Eickhout, B. et al. (2009), "The impact of environmental and climate constraints on global food supply", in *Economic Analysis of Land Use in Global Climate Change Policy*, edited by T. Hertel, S. Rose and R. Tol, Routledge, United States, www.routledge.com/products/9780415773089.

Havlík, P. et al. (2011), "Global land-use implications of first and second generation biofuel targets", *Energy Policy,* Vol. 39, pp. 5690-5702, Elsevier, www.sciencedirect.com/science/article/pii/S030142151000193X.

Havlík, P. et al. (2014), "Climate change mitigation through livestock system transitions", *Proceedings of the National Academy of Sciences of the United States of America*, Vol. 111, pp. 3709-3714, www.pnas.org/content/111/10/3709.full.

Rosegrant, M. W., and IMPACT Development Team (2012), *International Model for Policy Analysis of Agricultural Commodities and Trade (IMPACT) Model Description*, International Food Policy Research Institute, Washington D.C., http://ebrary.ifpri.org/cdm/ref/collection/p15738coll2/id/127162.

Van der Mensbrugghe, D. (2010), *The Environmental Impact and Sustainability Applied General Equilibrium (ENVISAGE) Model*, The World Bank, Washington, D.C., http://siteresources.worldbank.org/INTPROSPECTS/Resources/334934-1314986341738/Env7_1Jan10b.pdf.

Woltjer, G.B. and M. H. Kuiper (2014), *The MAGNET Model: Module Description*, LEI Report 14-057, LEI Wageningen UR (University & Research centre), Wageningen, http://edepot.wur.nl/310764.

Annex B

Quantification of scenarios and set-up of policy experiments

Quantification of scenarios

Quantifying the scenarios, which are outlined in qualitative terms, requires the generation of data for a variety of input variables for all regions covered by the different models. For practical reasons, and to avoid input data that are too far outside the space that can be reasonably expected, the data for variables driving the model results are generated on the basis of other existing scenarios, such as those developed by the International Panel on Climate change (IPCC) or other research organisations. Input data generated include the following key variables:

- Total population
- Per capita income (i.e. total GDP divided by total population)
- Productivity growth in agriculture, broken down into the following components:
  - Intrinsic crop yield growth
  - Intrinsic grassland yield growth
  - Feed conversion efficiency growth in livestock production
  - Effects of climate change on crop and grassland yields
- Energy and fertiliser prices
- First-generation biofuel policies
- Patterns of food demand
- Trade costs due to food market regulation differences

The three scenarios share similarities with some of the scenarios developed by the Intergovernmental Panel on Climate Change (IPCC) and can be linked to different emission pathways or Representative Concentration Pathways (RCPs). Specifically, the Individual, Fossil Fuel-Driven Growth scenario (also referred to as the "*Individual*" scenario for brevity) can be linked to the IPCC's Shared Socioeconomic Pathway SSP4 ("Inequality") combined with a moderate emission pathway RCP 4.5, the Citizen-Driven, Sustainable Growth scenario (or the "*Sustainable*" scenario in short) to the SSP1 ("Sustainability") combined with a low emission pathway RCP 2.6, and the Fast, Globally-Driven Growth scenario (or the "*Fast*" scenario) to the SSP5 ("Conventional Development"), combined with a high emission pathway 8.5.[1] For several of the drivers, however, the OECD scenarios differ from these IPCC ones. The required adjustments, the methods chosen and a brief overview of the resulting drivers are presented within this Annex.

Population growth

Population projections are based on the above-mentioned SSP scenarios, for which both population and GDP projections have been quantified (IIASA/OECD, 2013).

Figure B.1. Population assumptions by major regional groupings, 2010-2050

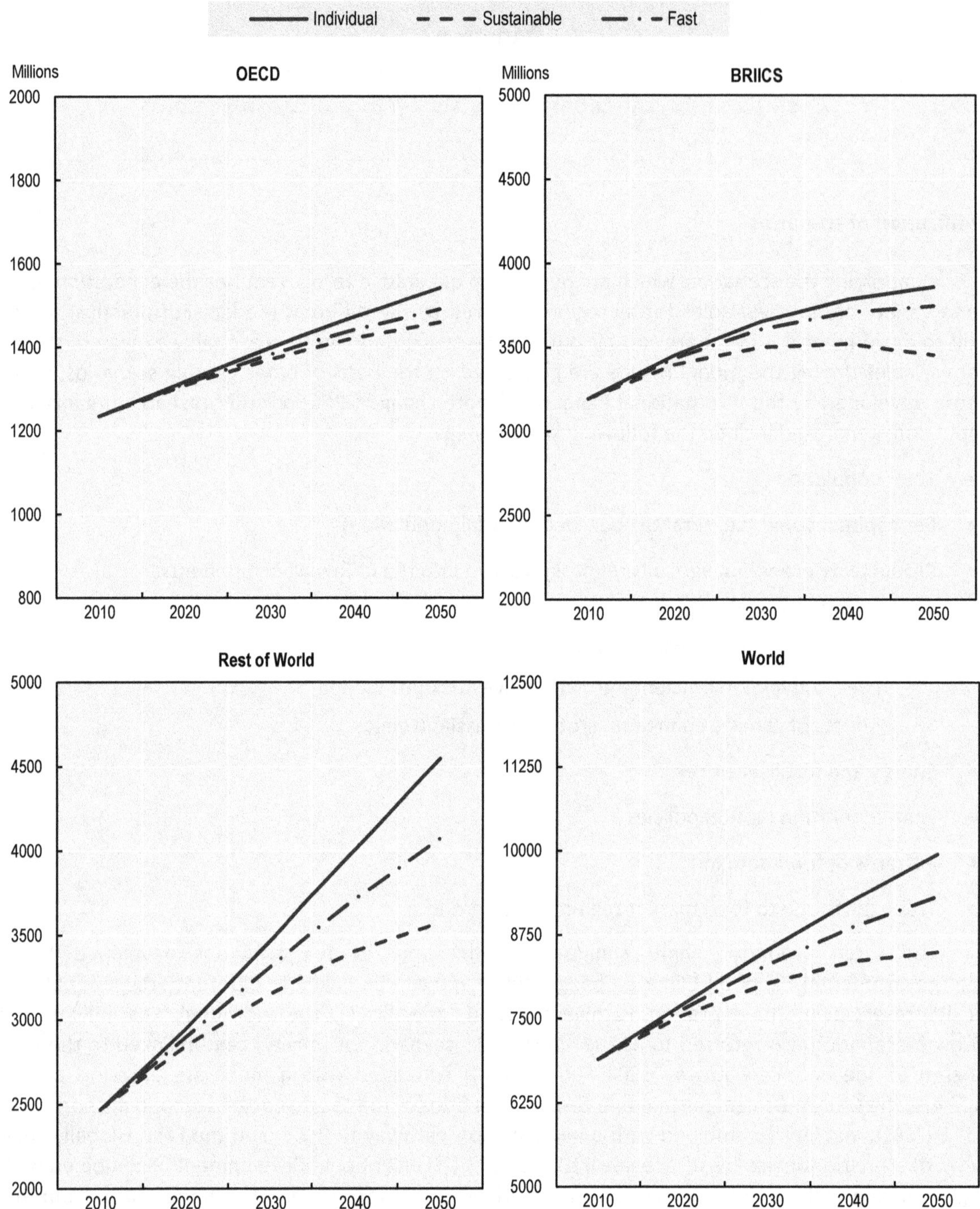

Note: OECD refers to the total of 34 OECD Member countries; BRIICS refers to the total of Brazil, Russian Federation, India, Indonesia, China and South Africa; Rest of World refers to the total of all other countries; World refers to the world total. Scales differ across panels.

Source: Calculated from IIASA/OECD (2013) based on the above formulas.

The *Individual* scenario assumes relatively higher population growth when compared to SSP4. As a consequence, population data for each region is calculated by using both the population data of SSP4 and that of another, higher-population scenario, based on the following formulas:

- For OECD countries: SSP4 * (1+ (SSP5/SSP4-1) * 0.7) [note that SSP5 is the highest population growth scenario for most OECD countries]
- For BRIICS countries: SSP4 * (1+ (SSP3/SSP4-1) * 0.7) [note that SSP3 is the highest population growth scenario for most BRIICS countries]
- For Rest of World (ROW) countries: SSP4 * (1+ (SSP3/SSP4-1) * 0.7) [note that SSP3 is the highest population growth scenario for ROW as an aggregate]

The *Sustainable* scenario is found to be sufficiently close to SSP1. As a result, population data from SSP1 is used for the *Sustainable* scenario without modifications.

The *Fast* scenario assumes relatively high population growth, although less than the *Individual* scenario. Consequently, the population data developed for SSP5 are adjusted based on the following formulas:

- For OECD countries: SSP5 * (1+ (SSP4/SSP5-1) * 0.5)
- For BRIICS countries: SSP5 * (1+ (SSP3/SSP5-1) * 0.5)
- For ROW countries: SSP5 * (1+ (SSP3/SSP5-1) * 0.5)

These adjustments correspond to the use of weighted averages between the main SSP scenario associated to the OECD one and another SSP scenario with comparatively high population growth. Figure B.1 shows the resulting population projections for the OECD, BRIICS and Rest of World. Total population in OECD countries is assumed to increase by between 18% and 25% between 2010 and 2050. Dominated by a shrinking China, the population of the BRIICS countries grows more slowly, by between 10% and 18%, and indeed falls between 2040 and 2050 in the *Sustainable* scenario. In contrast, the population of the Rest of the World is assumed to grow faster at between 45% and 84% between 2010 and 2050.

Per capita income growth

As with the case of population, income growth assumptions are based on the existing SSP scenarios. For the *Individual*, *Sustainable* and *Fast* scenarios, per capita GDP data are used directly from SSP4, SSP1 and SSP5, respectively, without any further adjustments.

Figure B.2, below, illustrates that per capita income growth differs more significantly than population across both regional groupings and across scenarios. Global per capita income is assumed to increase by between 117% and 181% between 2010 and 2050, with higher growth and larger differences across scenarios in BRIICS and Rest of World countries. In spite of significant income growth in both these regional groups, gaps relative to the OECD average remain significant: average incomes in the BRIICS countries reach between 21% and 32% of those within the current OECD by 2050, while those in the Rest of the World reach between 11% and 22%, an increase from 9% in 2010 for both regional groups.

Figure B.2. Per capita GDP assumptions by major regional groupings, 2010-2050

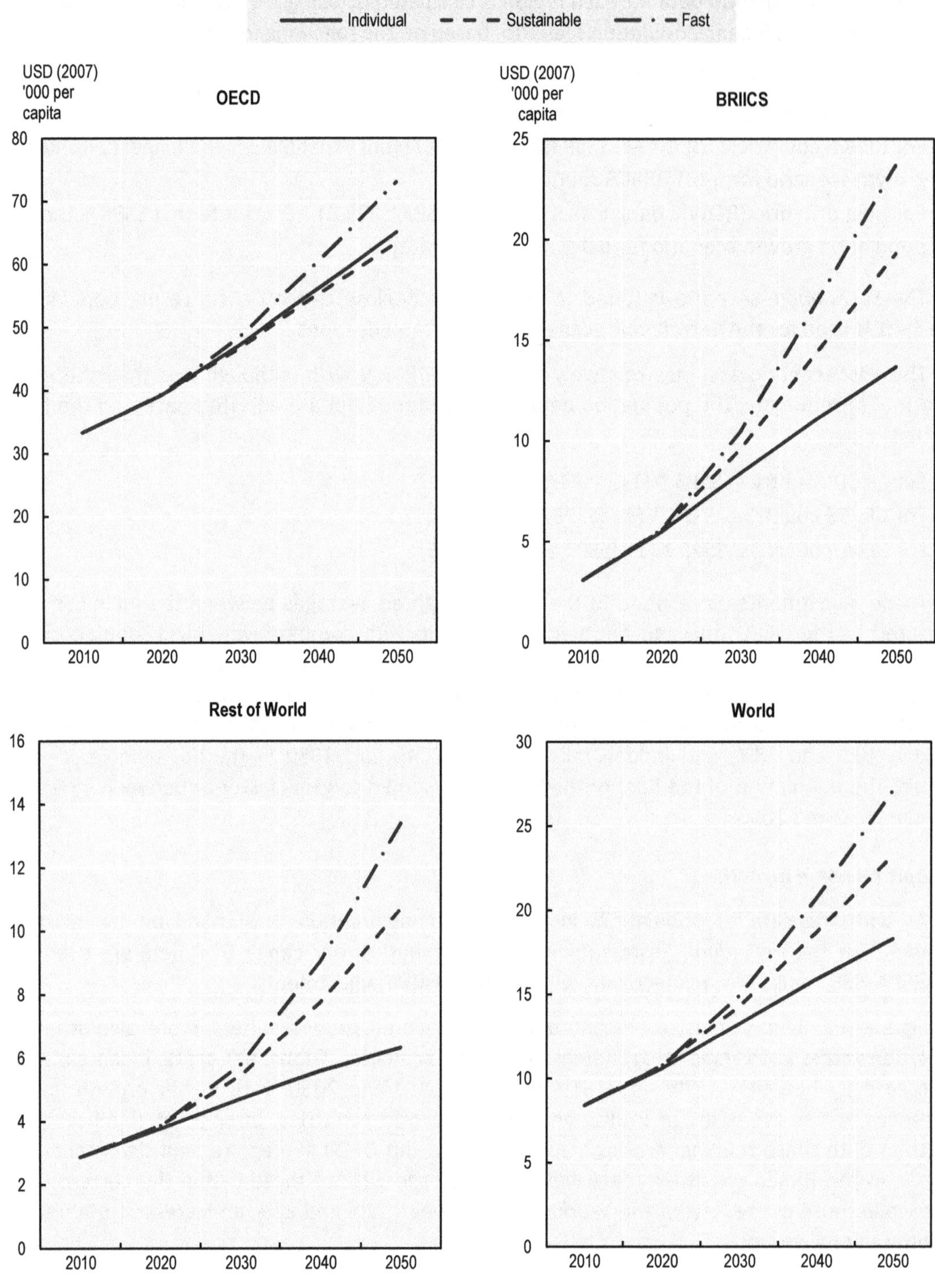

Notes: OECD refers to the total of 34 OECD member countries; BRIICS refers to the total of Brazil, Russian Federation, India, Indonesia, the people's Republic of China and South Africa; Rest of World refers to the total of all other countries; World refers to the world total. Incomes are measured in 2007 USD at market exchange rates. Scales differ across panels.

Source: Based on IIASA/OECD (2013).

Productivity growth in agriculture

Agricultural productivity is driven by a number of factors that can be represented by the models to different degrees. These include the following: i) intrinsic crop and grassland yield growth, as research and development activities drive technological developments which, together with possible environmental factors such as soil degradation, result in technologically determined changes in yields of both crop and grassland production; ii) feed conversion efficiency growth in livestock production, resulting from breeding and changes in production systems; and iii) the effects of climate change on crop and grassland yields. These elements are discussed separately below:

(i) Intrinsic crop and grassland yield growth

Changes in productivity in the crop sector are represented by "intrinsic productivity growth rates" (IPRs) as originally developed by the International Food Policy Research Institute (Nelson et al, 2010: 26). These IPRs, which can be interpreted as productivity growth due to technological change, environmental constraints etc., reflect historical trends in research expenditures, as well as expert judgements on future developments of research and management practices and their implications for crop yields. The IPRs have been updated to reflect the IPCC SSP2 (middle-of-the-road) scenario. Figure B.3 shows average crop IPRs by major production regions between 2010 and 2050. Generally speaking, these IPRs suggest that technology should result in crop yield growth that falls over time. However, differences across countries and crops are significant.

Figure B.3. Average intrinsic productivity growth rates (IPRs) for all crops, SSP2, 2010-2050

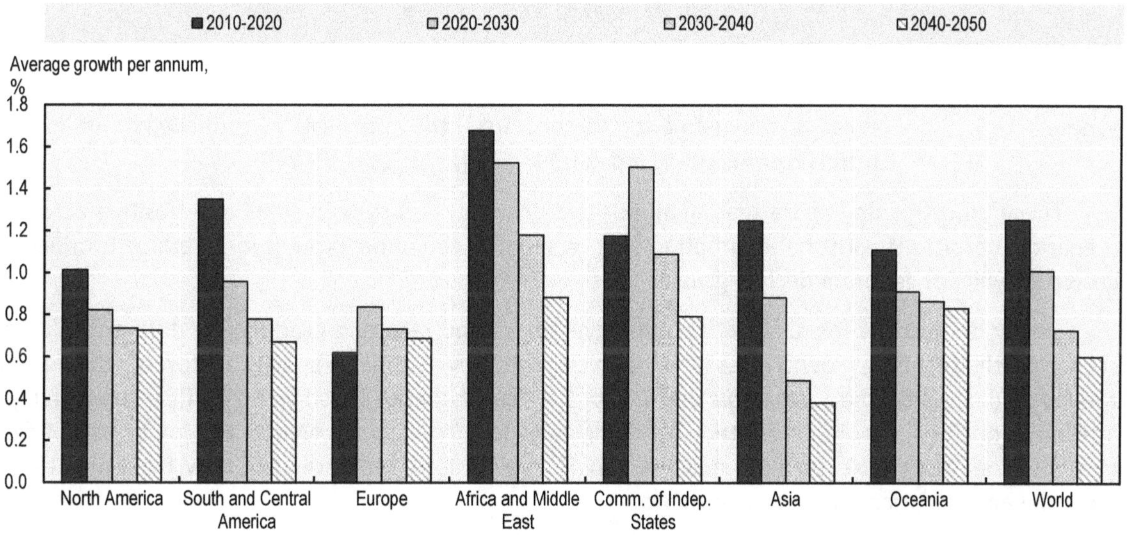

Source: provided by the International Food Policy Research Institute (IFPRI), May 2014.

Adjustments for other SSPs have been made, reflecting differences in countries' GDP. This follows the basic observation that higher GDP growth is correlated with higher expenditures for research and development (R&D) for agriculture, resulting in, among others, higher yield growth. These adjustments follow the following equation (Mason-D'Croz, 2014):

$$IPR_{s,r,i}^{t} = IPR_{SSP2,r,i}^{t} + \delta^{g} * \left(GDPGr_{s,r}^{t} - GDPGr_{SSP2,r}^{t}\right)$$

Where: IPR Intrinsic productivity growth rate
GDPGr GDP growth rate per year
δ^{g} sensitivity of IPRs to economic growth for country group g, where
$\delta^{dev'ed}$ = 0.05 for developed countries
δ^{BRIC} = 0.10 for Brazil, Russian Federation, India and China, and
$\delta^{dev'ing}$ = 0.20 for developing countries
t, s, r, i indices for time, scenario, region and crop, respectively

The methodology described above results in positive adjustments to productivity growth for high-growth scenarios, and conversely reduces productivity growth for low-growth scenarios. Essentially, the adjustments result in a symmetric change of the productivity index (where the index for 2005 is equal to 1) with the same adjustment factor for all crops in a country. IPR data for the three OECD scenarios, using the corresponding GDP assumptions, were equally generated in this way and provided by IFPRI.

However, for country-crop combinations with low or no intrinsic productivity growth for SSP2, these adjustments lead to negative productivity growth in some of the scenarios. The IPRs for the OECD scenarios were therefore modified such that adjustments relative to the productivity growth are multiplicative rather than additive:

Using the data provided by IFPRI, for each scenario, and separately by country, a relative adjustment factor *c* is calculated from the crop for which the productivity index is the highest:

$$c_{s,r}^{t} = \left(IPI_{s,r,i}^{t} - 1\right) / \left(IPI_{SSP2,r,i}^{t} - 1\right) \quad \text{for the i with the highest IPI}$$

$$IPI_{s,r,i}^{t} = c_{s,r}^{t} * \left(IPI_{SSP2,r,i}^{t} - 1\right) + 1 \quad \text{for all i}$$

Where: c Relative adjustment factor for the intrinsic productivity index
IPI Intrinsic productivity index ($IPI^{T} = \prod_{t=2006}^{T}(1 + IPR^{t})$)

These adjustments ensure that small positive growth rates remain small and positive across all scenarios, consistent with the assumption that, while low economic growth may reduce productivity growth, it will not generate declining yields.

Finally, to account for different technology choices and resulting productivity differences across scenarios, the resulting growth rates have been corrected by a scenario-specific factor, equal to 1.4 for the *Individual*, 0.9 for the *Sustainable* and 1.2 for the *Fast* scenario. These factors reflect the high input intensity and fossil fuel input-related technologies in the *Individual* scenario, the lower use of farm inputs in the *Sustainable* scenario and the rapid development and spread of new technologies and high coal and gas prices in the *Fast* scenario.

GLOBIOM uses a slightly different set of IPRs for the three scenarios based on an extrapolation of past historical trends on the basis of the evolution of GDP per capita in the different regions. Crop yields were fitted on national log GDP per capita over the period 1980-2009 in a fixed effects panel estimation. A separate dummy was created for country grouping by GDP category, using the World Bank categories with slight changes in group thresholds to balance groups and have enough observations in each group. A separate estimate was made for each of the 18 crops. Formally, the fixed effects model is:

$$y_{it}^{c} = \sum_{g}^{G} s_{ig}\beta_{g}^{c} x_{it} + \alpha_{i} + u_{it}$$

where y_{it}^{c} shows country i's yield of crop c in period t, coefficient β_{g}^{c} captures the effect of GDP per capita of countries in group g, s_{ig} stands for the GDP per capita group dummy with $s_{ig} = 1 \; \forall \; i \in g$ (i.e. if country i belongs to GDP per capita group g), α_{i} captures the countries' individual time-invariant difference, and u_{it} denotes the unobserved error term. IPRs growth rate are then projected using the GDP per capita projections associated to each of the scenarios (IIASA, 2013).

Growth rates for grassland yields have been generated based on the same methodology, but using default yield growth rates provided by The Netherlands Environmental Assessment Agency (PBL), which are taken as related to the middle-of-the-road SSP2 scenario. Grassland productivity is based on dry matter yields per hectare. The corresponding growth rates had been developed within the IMAGE modelling system to match FAO's "Agriculture Towards 2050" projections (FAO, 2012). It is assumed that half of this growth relates to technical progress, corresponding to the IPRs in crop production, while the remaining half is linked to market-induced changes in grass yields, hence not considered in the generation of grass IPRs. As for crop IPRs, the grass IPRs have been adjusted according to both GDP differences and technology assumptions for the three OECD scenarios. Figure B.5 shows the resulting growth rates for the examples of Oceania (upper panel) and Western Africa (lower panel), the regions with the lowest and highest growth in grassland productivity. Note that apart from R&D expenditures, differences across regions are influenced by a range of factors, including current productivity levels and changes in livestock production systems.

Figure B.4. Average global IPRs for all crops, 2010-2050

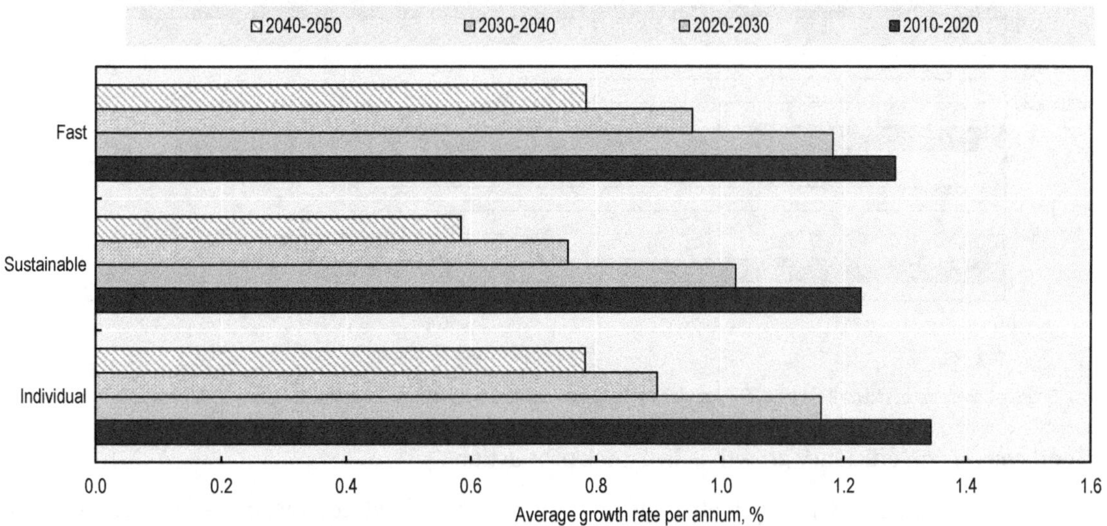

Source: Calculated from IPRs for SSPs as provided by the International Food Policy Research Institute (IFPRI), May 2014.

Figure B.5. Average IPRs for grassland, Oceania (upper panel) and Brazil (lower panel), OECD scenarios and SSP2, 2010-2050

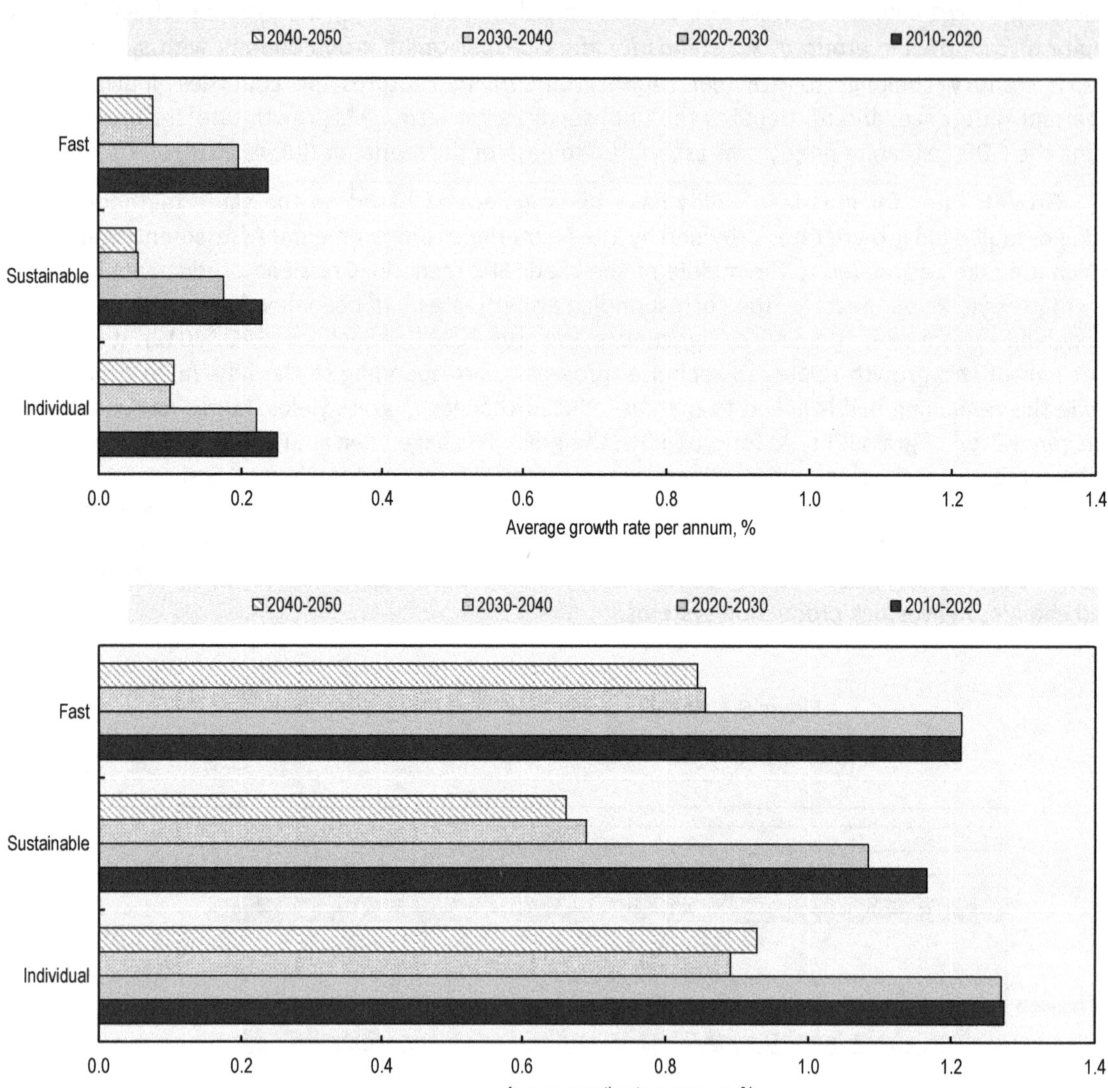

Source: Calculated based on IPRs for SSP2 provided by The Netherlands Environmental Assessment Agency (PBL), May 2014.

ii) Feed conversion efficiency growth in livestock production

Similar to grassland productivity, information on total feed conversion efficiency was kindly provided by PBL, prepared in such a way as to reproduce the long-term projections of FAO (2012). Feed use ratios, expressed as livestock production divided by feed use, have been provided for five groups of livestock and for five different types of feed. For the purpose of the OECD scenarios, these data have been aggregated into two livestock types, ruminant and non-ruminant, as well as across all types of feed. Distributional changes are more likely related to market and price effects than to technological developments, while these latter – together with changes in production systems – mainly affect the total feed requirement for producing a unit of livestock products.

Figure B.6. Average growth rates in total feed efficiency, Russian Federation and neighbouring countries (upper panel) and East Africa (lower panel), OECD scenarios and SSP2, 2010-2050

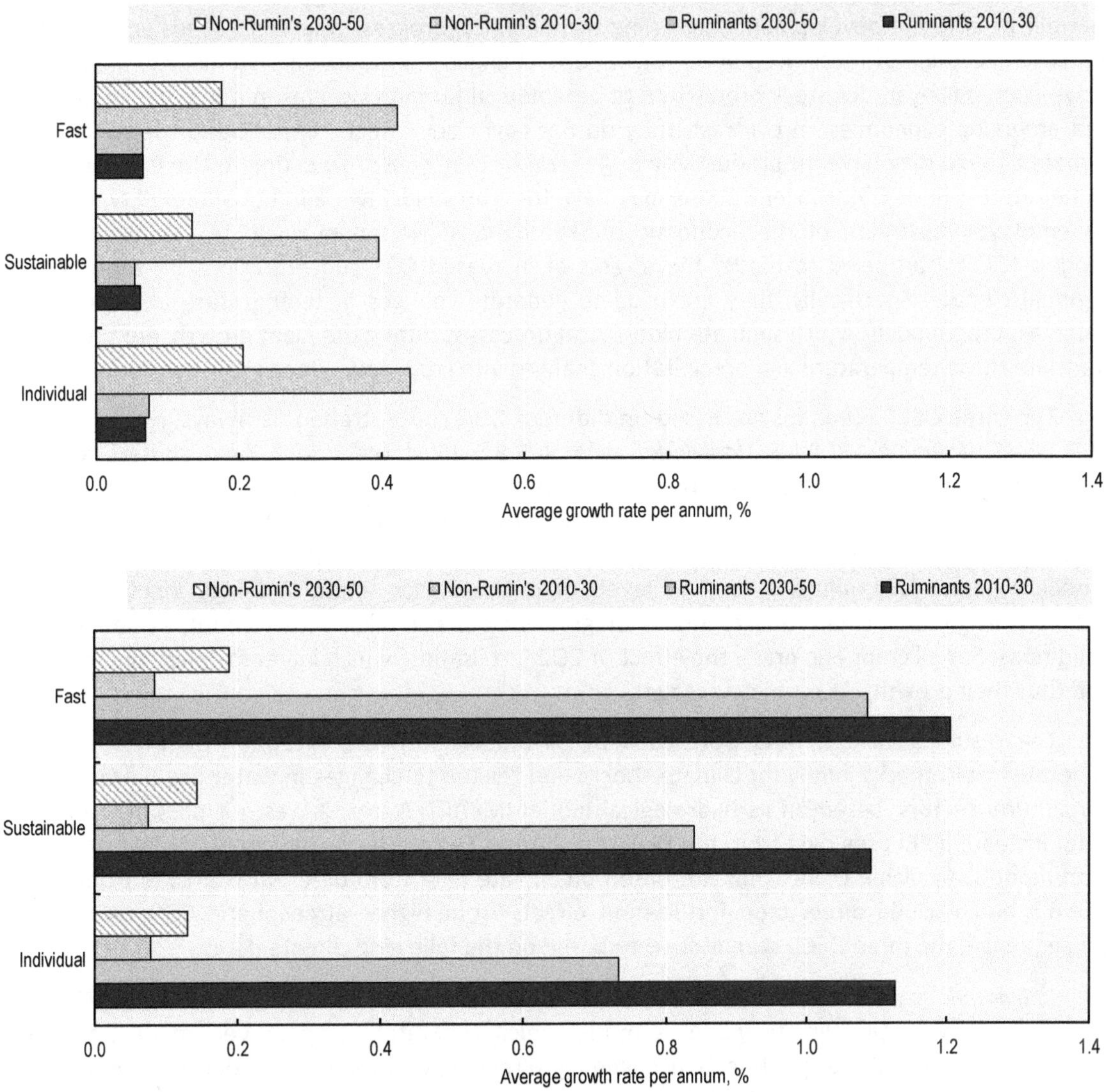

Source: Calculated based on IPRs for SSP2 provided by The Netherlands Environmental Assessment Agency (PBL), May 2014.

The resulting growth rates in feed use efficiency, expressed in kg of livestock products per kg of feed, which again are taken to hold for a middle-of-the-road SSP2 scenario, were adjusted for the different OECD scenarios, based on the same methodology. Figure B.6 shows the resulting growth rates for two regional aggregates, with the Russian Federation and neighbouring countries showing lowest growth in the ruminant sector, and East Africa showing the highest rates in that sector.

GLOBIOM is based on a disaggregated representation of livestock systems, therefore conversion efficiency rates have to be implemented at the livestock system level. Trends in feed efficiency per system are estimated within GLOBIOM using an extrapolation of historical observation. First, global annual rates of the increase in feed conversion efficiency were estimated for livestock products from Soussana et al. (2012) for SSP2; second, regional and SSP-specific annual rates of increase were calculated by scaling this central estimate by the rates of change estimated for crop yields as described above for GLOBIOM crop IPRs projections. Where necessary, a ceiling was fixed to avoid biologically infeasible values (IIASA, 2013).

iii) Effects of climate change on crop and grassland yields

The productivity growth rates projected along the methodology outlined above combine a number of different developments, including technological progress related to seeds and breeds but, with the exception of those used in GLOBIOM, also changes in production systems, e.g. the continued move from back-yard livestock production to commercial farming systems in a number of developing and emerging economies. In contrast, they do not cover any effects, beneficial or detrimental, that climate change may have on productivity in general or crop yields. To estimate the implications that higher atmospheric CO2 concentrations may have for crop yields, two additional model types need to be employed upstream of the economic market models (Nelson et al., 2014). Global Circulation Models (GCMs) are used to model the effects of increased CO2 concentrations on the global and regional climate. Specifically, they are used to generate changes in temperature and precipitation patterns. Crop models, which simulate biophysical processes during the plant growth, are then used to translate these temperature and precipitation changes into crop yield effects.

The three OECD scenarios are based on different GHG concentration pathways, corresponding to RCP 2.6 (*Sustainable*), RCP 4.5 (*Individual*) and RCP 8.5 (*Fast* scenario).[2] Yield shifters are kindly provided by IIASA, based on simulations with the Environmental Policy Integrated Climate (EPIC) Model and using temperature and precipitation data generated by the HadGEM2-ES General Circulation Model (GCM).[3] Yield impacts are calculated for each of the 18 crops used by the GLOBIOM model, automatically adjusting for two levels of fertilisers, low input and high input, and, where available, irrigation. Climate change impact on grass yield is also taken into account, assuming rain-fed conditions. For all crops and grass, the effect of CO2 fertilisation, which increases plant photosynthesis and thus their growth, is taken into account.

The resulting yield shifters were used by all models with the exception of IMPACT: as IFPRI generates yield shocks jointly for climate shocks and related to changes in water use patterns in non-agricultural sectors, based on its hydrological model IMPACT-Water, it was not possible to use EPIC data. Instead, IFPRI uses data from the Decision Support System for Agrotechnology Transfer (DSSAT) crop models. Available DSSAT runs are based on climate data from different GCMs, but only include RCP 8.5 and exclude direct crop fertilisation effects from higher atmospheric CO2 content. As a consequence, the three OECD scenarios were based on the following climate data:

- *Individual* scenario: RCP 8.5 based on climate data from the Geophysical Fluid Dynamics Laboratory (GFDL) climate model, a model which generates comparatively modest changes in temperature and precipitation, hence leading to relatively moderate yield declines overall.
- *Sustainable* scenario: No yield shocks from climate change assumed.
- *Fast* scenario: RCP 8.5 based on climate data from the UK Met Office's Hadley Center Global Environment Model version 2 (HadGEM2), a model which generates comparatively large changes in temperature and precipitation, hence leading to relatively strong yield declines overall.

Energy and fertiliser prices

Energy price projections are taken from the IEA's *World Energy Outlook* (IEA, 2013). The *World Energy Outlook* specifies price projections towards 2035 for a number of fossil energies. The OECD scenarios make use of the "Current Policy Scenario" projections for the prices of crude oil (IEA crude oil import price), natural gas (natural gas prices for North America, Europe, and the Pacific regions), and coal (OECD steam coal import price). The distinction of regional gas prices appears important as recent natural gas prices in North America have fallen significantly relative to other regions as well as relative to crude oil and coal, following the large-scale fracking of shale gas, notably in the United

States. While the spread is assumed to shrink over time, Pacific gas prices are still twice as high as North American gas prices in 2050.

The projections for the "Current Policy Scenario", extended until 2050, were used unmodified for the *Individual* scenario. In comparison, while maintaining the regional differentiation for natural gas prices, energy prices in the *Sustainable* scenario were assumed higher notably in the medium term, with 2030 prices for crude oil 14% higher than in the *Individual* scenario, a difference falling to 4% towards 2050 as alternative forms of energy become more competitive.

Finally, the *Fast* scenario not only assumes somewhat lower energy prices, but sees the spread across regions as well as across different fuel types fall by half until 2050. As a consequence, while oil prices are assumed to be one-third lower in the *Fast* scenario than in the *Individual* one by 2050, North American gas prices are assumed to be 25% higher in the same year. Final energy price assumptions are shown in Figure B.7.

Figure B.7. Energy prices for different forms of fossil energy, historical 2000-2012 and assumptions towards 2050

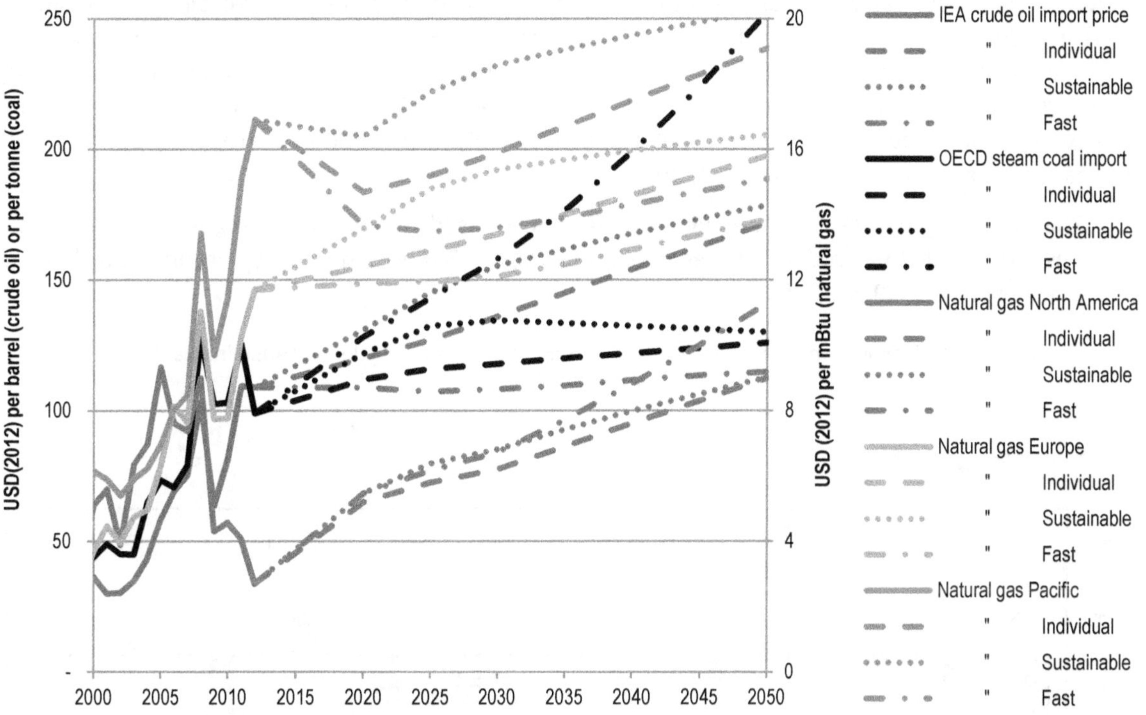

Source: IEA (2013); own calculations.

Most important for agriculture, these energy prices drive price levels for fertilisers. Fertiliser price projections are developed from prices for crude oil, natural gas and coal using cost shares of different types of energy in fertiliser production. These cost shares, extracted from the MAGNET database, have been kindly provided by the Dutch Agricultural Economics Research Institute LEI-WUR (Bartelings, 2014). Globally, energy accounts for about 21% of fertiliser production costs, mostly natural gas but also – particularly in the case of China – coal. Regional shares differ significantly, however. Shares are driven particularly by the type of fertiliser principally produced in a region: while phosphorus and potash are to a large extent mined products with little-to-moderate processing, nitrogen fertilisers are highly energy-intensive products.

First-generation biofuel policies

All contextual scenarios assume current legislation on first-generation biofuels to be maintained throughout the projection period. This mainly relates to mandated biofuel shares or volumes in the transportation sector. Due to the different implementation of biofuels across models, final biofuel production and use – and hence the use of feedstock crops – can, however, differ.

Patterns of food demand

Food consumption of individual agricultural products is not predefined across models, but result mainly from population and income growth (see above). However, the *Sustainable* scenario explicitly assumes a shift in preferences in favour of more "sustainable" diets. Corresponding shifters have been provided by the International Institute for Applied Systems Analysis (IIASA) and are based on a number of key assumptions. First, reflecting better management of domestic waste in developed countries, per capita consumption of food has stabilised in most advanced economies. Second, individuals evolve towards healthier diets, balanced in calories and proteins. Regions with total protein consumption above 75 grams per capita per day reduce their level of meat consumption. Protein from ruminant meat is reduced to a maximum of five grams per capita of day. At the same time, regions with less than 25 grams of protein per capita per day increase their consumption of non-ruminant meat, resulting in increased livestock production in a number of developing countries. Because these regions reduce their dependence on low nutrient food, per capita consumption of root products is also decreased below 100 kcal per day (IIASA, 2013).

The shifters generated and provided by IIASA are based on relative changes in consumption patterns and detailed by product and regional group. Figure B.8 presents these consumption shifts at the global level for 2030 and 2050.[4]

Figure B.8. Global changes in consumption of different food groups due to "sustainable diets", 2030 and 2050

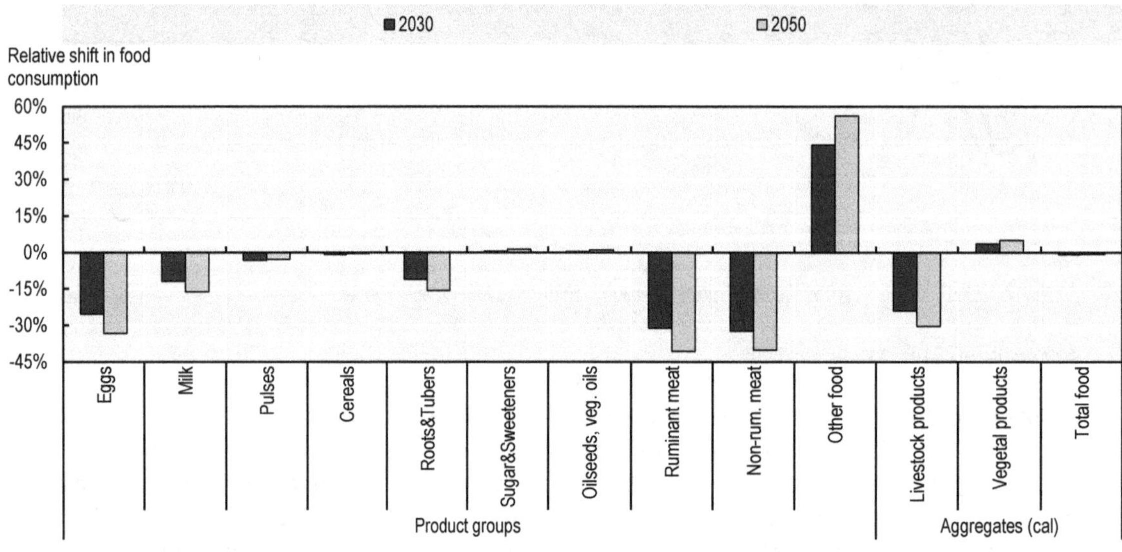

Source: Shifters provided by the International Institute for Applied Systems Analysis (IIASA), 2014.

Trade costs due to food market regulation differences

Differences in food market regulations can result in increased costs for the trade of agricultural products across countries and regions. As the models used for quantifying the OECD scenarios do not specifically account for costs related to such differences, alternative assumptions were made for the scenarios and represented as Iceberg costs. For this purpose, and to represent the regionalisation embedded in two of the three scenarios, the world is divided into three large blocks, including i) The Americas, ii) Europe, Middle East and Africa, and iii) Asia and Oceania.

Compared to the *Sustainable* scenario, for which no changes in regulation-related trade costs are assumed, the *Individual* scenario features an increase in Iceberg costs by 10% for trade in food and agriculture between these three large blocks, but no change for trade *within* the blocks. In contrast, the *Fast* scenario assumes a decrease in Iceberg costs for trade in food and agriculture between any two modelled regions by 10%. These changes are assumed to occur in a linear development between 2010 and 2030, with no further changes between 2030 and 2050.

Set-up of policy experiments

Development of a "greener lifestyle"

The development of a "green lifestyle", arising from greater awareness of environmental and health concerns, will involve a number of different facets. First, it involves changes in food consumption to become healthier and more sustainable. Second, it involves increased efforts to protect biodiversity and rich ecosystems. These are detailed below:

- **Changes in food consumption:** Food consumption is assumed to shift towards healthier and more sustainable patterns. The policy experiment assumes changes in food demand along the lines already implemented for the *Sustainable* scenario, i.e. a reduction of domestic waste, reductions in the consumption of animal products in regions of high protein intake, and an increase in protein intake from animal products in developing countries. See "Patterns of food demand" in the "Quantification of scenarios" section above.

- **Increased biodiversity protection:** The expansion of agriculture and forest plantations is prevented in rich ecosystems areas. Protected areas correspond to those already identified as protected under the WCMC-UNEP database, but also to other biodiversity hotspots identified by environmental organisations. The implementation of these data within GLOBIOM follows Kraxner et al. (2013). A conversion restriction is applied in each unit of the model where a biodiversity sensitive area is identified. These sensitive areas are defined through the use of the following biodiversity maps: i) WWF Global 200 Ecoregions (Olson and Dinerstein, 2002); ii) WWF/IUCN Centres of Plant Diversity (WWF/IUCN, 1994); iii) Amphibian Diversity Areas (Duellman, 1999); iv) Conservational International's Hotspots (Mittermeier et al., 2004); v) Birdlife International Endemic Bird Areas (BirdLife International, 2008); and vi) Alliance for Zero Extinctions Sites (Ricketts et al., 2005). This significantly restricts the extent of natural land – forest and wetlands included – that could be converted globally from 7 Gha to 1.5 Gha. Of course, only a minor part of this land can in practice be used for agriculture, due to climate and soil suitability consideration, effective accessibility to population and markets, and other possible conflicting uses of land, including additional conservation provisions.

Figure B.9. Natural land (forest, wetlands, natural vegetation) available for conversion with and without protection

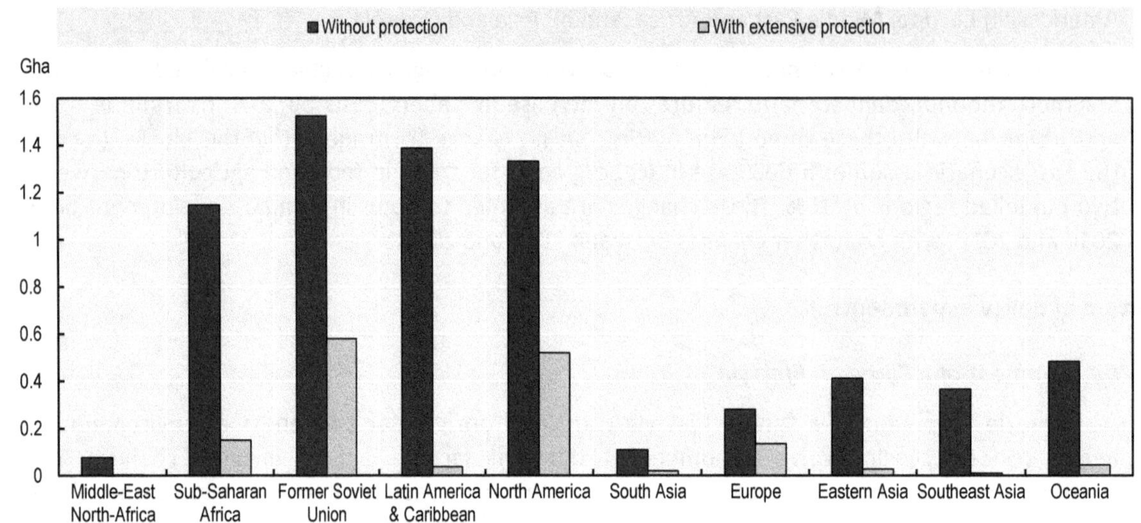

Source: IIASA, adapted from Kraxner et al. (2013).

Improved coherence of food market regulations

The improved coherence of food market regulations is represented by reductions in tariff equivalents for trade in agricultural and food products. As outlined above, trade costs related to differences in food market regulations are assumed to develop differently for the three contextual scenarios. Given that the starting points for the policy experiments are different, the assumed changes in trade costs must also differ.

- Under the *Individual* scenario, an improved coherence of food market regulations is approximated by a 15% reduction in trade costs for trade between the three large regional blocks, outlined above. For trade within the blocks, a reduction of 5% is assumed. For the *Sustainable* scenario, a general 10% reduction in trade costs is assumed for all trade relations. Finally, in the *Fast* scenario, a further 5% reduction in the trade costs for all trade flows is assumed on top of the already lower costs related to reducing differences in food market regulations in this scenario. These numbers are in line with Dee et al. (2011).

All of these changes are assumed to follow a linear development between 2025 and 2035, with no further changes in regulation-related trade costs after 2035.

Improved infrastructure

The improvement of infrastructure – both physical, such as paving roads, and information and communication systems – leads to reduced costs for the conversion of an agricultural primary product on farm to a final food product consumed by the end user. The experiment is therefore based on the cost shares of final food products that are attributable to infrastructure-related cost elements, notably transportation and other similar services, as well as retail. These costs are taken from the GTAP database and shown, for selected products and regions, in Figure B.10.

Figure B.10. Infrastructure-related costs for selected products and regions, share in total product values

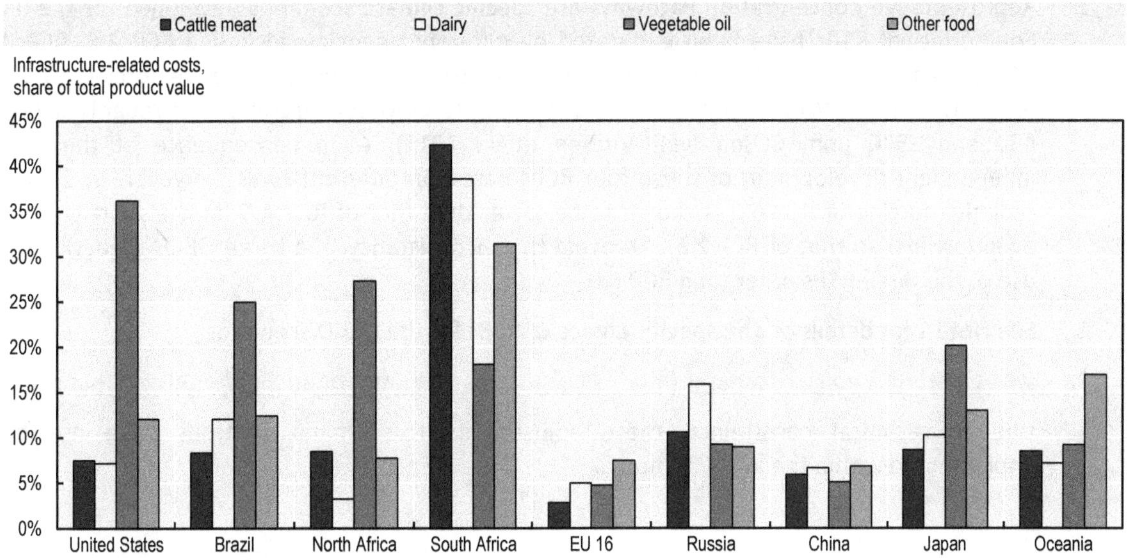

Source: GTAP Database, GTAP version 8.1 (February 2013).

As infrastructure-related obstacles are important in the developing world in particular, the related costs are assumed to decline by 20% in Africa, and South and Southeast Asia. For Latin America, a reduction by 10% is assumed. Infrastructural improvements are less urgent in the developed world, where the transportation system is generally much better. The experiment therefore assumes a reduction of infrastructure-related costs by only 5% for these countries.

Similar to the experiment on food-related regulations, the cost reductions are implemented in a linear way between 2025 and 2035, with no further changes after 2035.

Sustainable productivity growth

The area of green methods and technologies can involve a broad range of changes. Two options were chosen, resulting in two separate policy experiments. The first looks at improvements in the efficiency of water use in agricultural irrigation systems, combined with an expansion of irrigated land, while the second analyses the implications of new crop varieties that would allow the offsetting of a part of the climate change-induced reduction of average crop yields:

- **Improved and expanded agricultural irrigation:** Irrigation in agriculture accounts for the majority of global freshwater use, and a number of regions face shortages in water supplies. Expanding irrigation is therefore often only possible to the extent that water use efficiency within the irrigation systems can be improved. Based on the hydrological information available at IFPRI and IIASA, this policy experiment assumes a 20% increase in water use efficiency. The water savings from this higher efficiency are assumed to be re-utilised by expanded irrigation areas.
- **Climate change-resilient crop varieties:** This experiment assumes the availability of crop varieties that are more resistant to climate change-related stresses, such as draughts and pests. Three key crops are considered, including wheat, maize – coarse grains where maize is not singled out – and rice. Based on the individual contextual scenarios, a reduction by one-third of climate change-related yield damages is assumed. In cases where climate change results in no or positive yield effects, this experiment assumes no yield changes from the new varieties.

Notes

1. Representative Concentration Pathways are specific climate scenarios developed for the IPCC. Four principal RCPs have been generated by different agencies, including RCP 2.6, RCP 4.5, RCP 6.0 and RCP 8.5. The numbers correspond to the assumed radiative forcing by 2100 (i.e. between 2.6 W/m^2 and 8.5 W/m^2) and relate to GHG concentrations of roughly between 490 and 1370 ppm CO_2eq (van Vuuren et al., 2011). As a consequence of the largely independent development of these four RCPs based on different tools, however, by 2050 the radiative forcing of RCP 6.0 is shown to be lower than that of RCP 4.5 (in the short term, it is even lower than that of RCP 2.6). To avoid this inconsistency, the three OECD scenarios make use of the three RCPs other than RCP 6.0.

2. See Note 1 for details on the specific choice of RCPs for the OECD scenarios.

3. www.metoffice.gov.uk/research/modelling-systems/unified-model/climate-models/hadgem2.

4. Due to technical constraints, these adjustments to demand patterns have not been implemented within the IMPACT model.

Annex B References

Bartelings, H. (2014), Personal email communication, April 2014.

BirdLife International (2008), *Endemic Bird Areas*, BirdLife International, www.birdlife.org/datazone/sowb/casestudy/76.

Dee, P. et al. (2011), "The impact of trade liberalisation on jobs and growth: Technical note", *OECD Trade Policy Working Papers*, No. 107, OECD Publishing, Paris, http://dx.doi.org/10.1787/5kgj4jfj1nq2-en.

Duellman, W.E. (ed.) (1999), *Patterns of Distribution of Amphibians: A Global Perspective*, John Hopkins University Press, Baltimore.

FAO (2012), *World Agriculture Towards 2030/2050: The 2012 Revision*, ESA Working Paper No. 12/03. Food and Agriculture Organization, Rome, www.fao.org/docrep/016/ap106e/ap106e.pdf.

GTAP (2013), *GTAP Version 8.1* (database), published February 2013, www.gtap.agecon.purdue.edu/databases/v8/default.asp (accessed July 2014).

IEA (2013), *World Energy Outlook 2013*, International Energy Agency, Paris, www.worldenergyoutlook.org/weo2013.

IIASA (2013), "Preliminary scenarios of the developments in agricultural commodity markets, livestock production systems, and land use and land cover (Deliverable 2.2)", *AnimalChange*, www.iiasa.ac.at/web/home/research/researchPrograms/EcosystemsServicesandManagement/D2.2 AnimalChange.pdf.

IIASA/OECD (2013), SSP Database (version 0.93), https://secure.iiasa.ac.at/web-apps/ene/SspDb/dsd?Action=htmlpage&page=welcome (accessed April 2014).

Kraxner, F. et al. (2013), "Global bioenergy scenarios: Future forest development, land-use implications, and trade-offs", *Biomass and Bioenergy,* Vol. 57, pp. 86-96. http://dx.doi.org/10.1016/j.biombioe.2013.02.003.

Mason-D'Croz, D. (2014), Personal email communication, June 2014.

Mittermeier, R.A. et al. (2004), *Hotspots Revisited: Earth's Biologically Richest and Most Endangered Terrestrial Ecoregions*, Arlington VI: Conservation International, University of Chicago Press, www.press.uchicago.edu/ucp/books/book/distributed/H/bo3707156.html.

Nelson, G.C. et al. (2010), *Food Security, Farming, and Climate Change to 2050 – Scenarios, Results, Policy Options*, International Food Policy Research Institute, Washington, D.C., www.ifpri.org/sites/default/files/publications/rr172.pdf.

Nelson, G.C. et al. (2014), "Climate change effects on agriculture: Economic responses to biophysical shocks", *Proceedings of the National Academy of Sciences of the United States of America*, Vol. 111, pp. 3274-3279, www.pnas.org/content/early/2013/12/12/1222465110.abstract.

Olson, D.M. and E. Dinerstein (2002), "The global 200: Priority ecoregions for global conservation", *Annals of the Missouri Botanical Garden,* Vol. 89, pp.199-224. www.worldwildlife.org/publications/the-global-200-priority-ecoregions-for-global-conservation.

Ricketts, T.H. et al. (2005), "Pinpointing and preventing imminent extinctions", *Proceedings of the National Academy of Sciences of the United States of America*, Vol. 102/51, pp.18497-18501, www.pnas.org/content/102/51/18497.abstract.

Soussana, J.F. et. al (2012), "Storylines for the livestock sector scenarios in EU, studied SICA regions and global level (Deliverable 2.1)", *AnimalChange*, INRA, Paris, www.animalchange.eu/Docs/Deliverables/D2.1%20Storylines%20for%20livestock%20sector%20scenarios.pdf.

Van Vuuren, D.P. et al. (2011), "The representative concentration pathways: An overview", *Climate Change*, Vol. 109, pp. 5-31, http://link.springer.com/content/pdf/10.1007%2Fs10584-011-0148-z.pdf.

WWF/IUCN (1994), *Centres of Plant Diversity: A Guide and Strategy for their Conservation*, World Wide Fund for Nature and International Union for Conservation of Nature, Cambridge.

Annex C

Additional results from the scenario quantification

Figure C.1. Per capita food availability in developed countries, 1970-2050

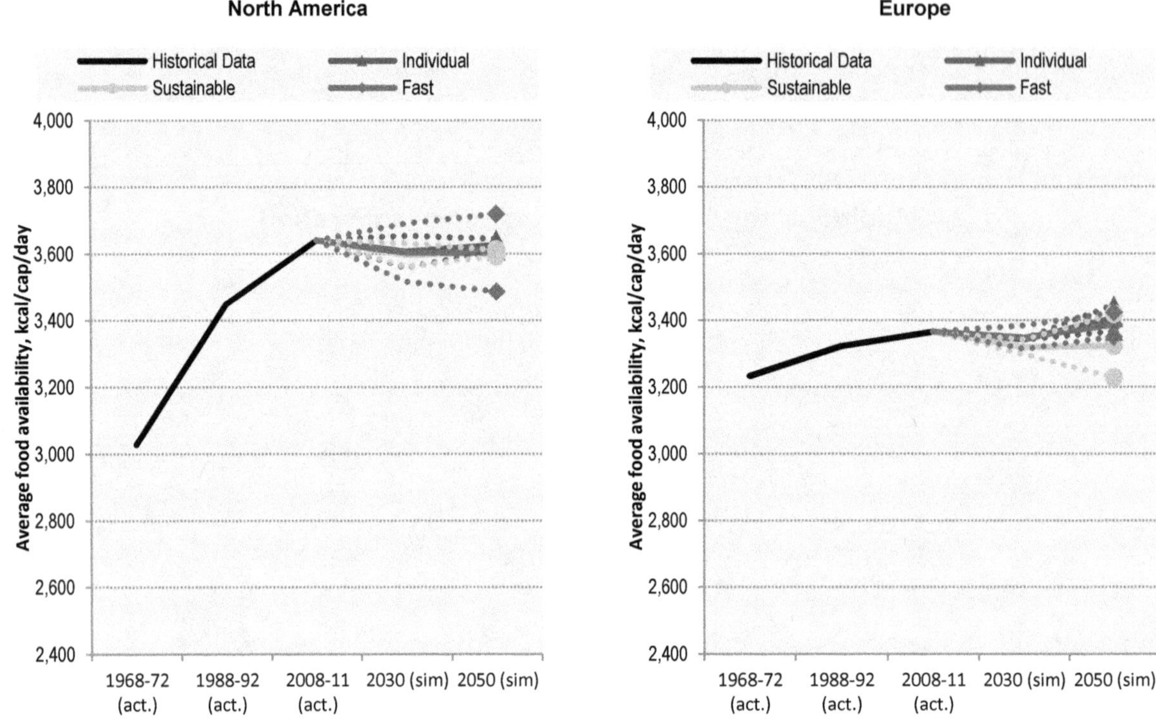

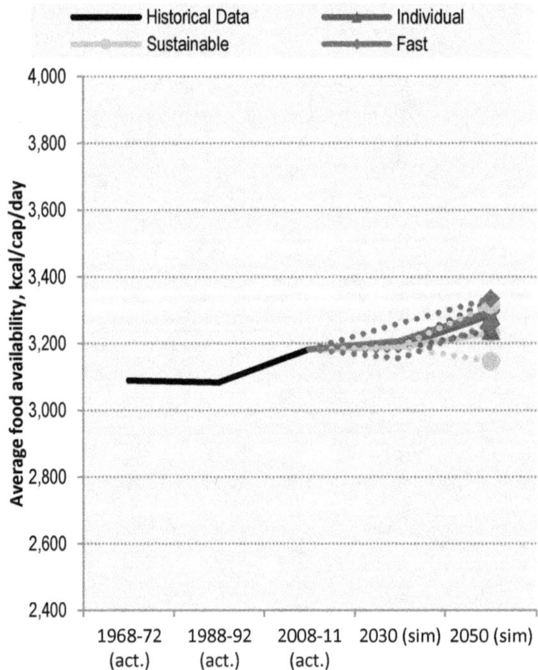

Note: Thick lines represent means across the two PE models providing calorie data, while dotted lines represent the range of model results (minima and maxima). Model results are relative changes in time between 2010, 2030 and 2050, superimposed on actual data from other sources, so prospects in levels are derived from additional calculations.

Source: Historical data from FAOSTAT (2014); prospects from results provided by contributing models.

Figure C.2. Crop and pasture land cover, 1970-2050: world total and selected regions

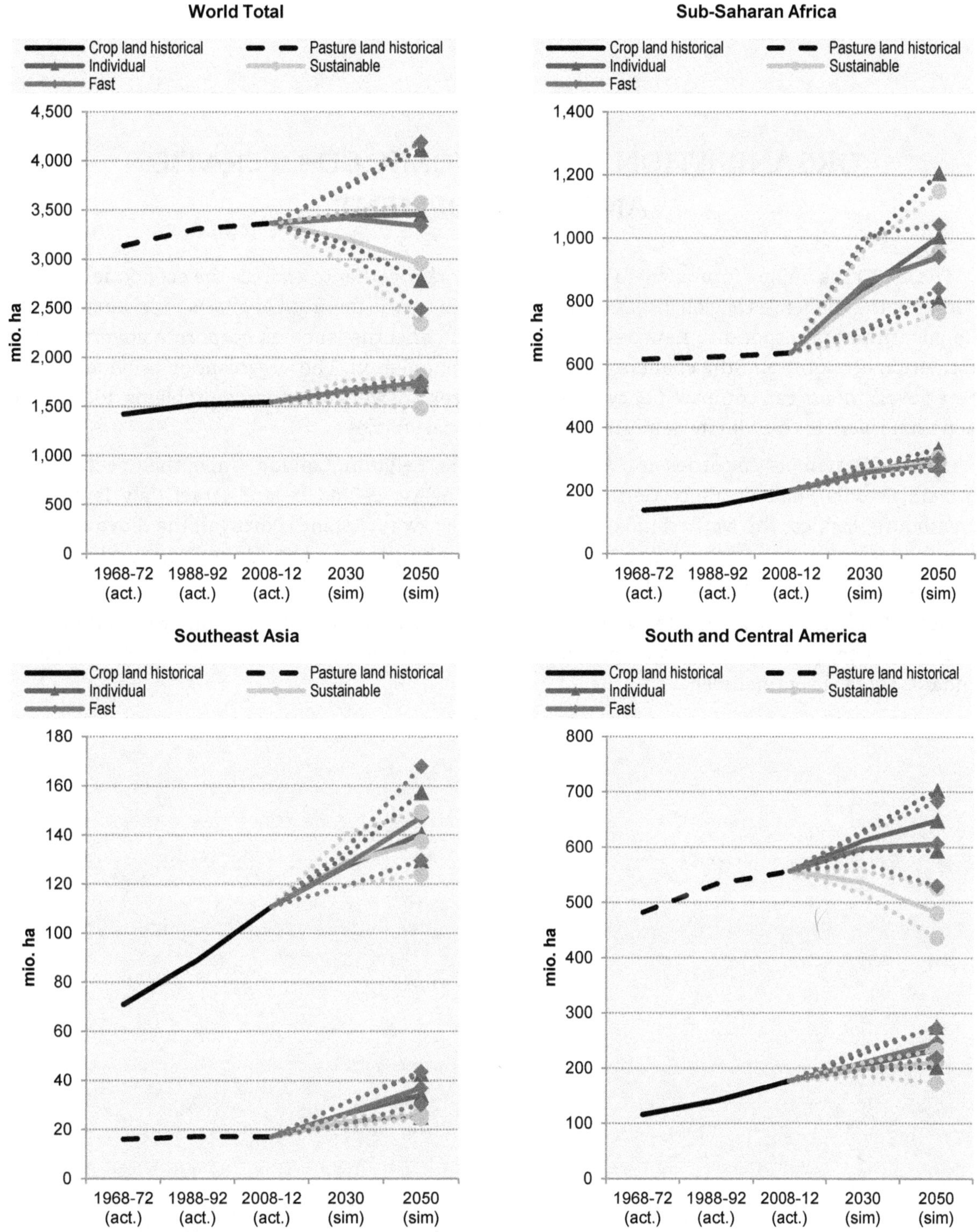

Note: Model results are relative changes in time between 2010, 2030 and 2050, superimposed on actual data from other sources, so prospects in levels are derived from additional calculations. Thick lines represent means across the three models providing agricultural land use data, while dotted lines represent the range of model results (minima and maxima). Projections on pasture area provided by ENVISAGE and MAGNET only.

Source: Historical data from FAOSTAT (2014); prospects from results provided by contributing models.

ORGANISATION FOR ECONOMIC CO-OPERATION AND DEVELOPMENT

The OECD is a unique forum where governments work together to address the economic, social and environmental challenges of globalisation. The OECD is also at the forefront of efforts to understand and to help governments respond to new developments and concerns, such as corporate governance, the information economy and the challenges of an ageing population. The Organisation provides a setting where governments can compare policy experiences, seek answers to common problems, identify good practice and work to co-ordinate domestic and international policies.

The OECD member countries are: Australia, Austria, Belgium, Canada, Chile, the Czech Republic, Denmark, Estonia, Finland, France, Germany, Greece, Hungary, Iceland, Ireland, Israel, Italy, Japan, Korea, Luxembourg, Mexico, the Netherlands, New Zealand, Norway, Poland, Portugal, the Slovak Republic, Slovenia, Spain, Sweden, Switzerland, Turkey, the United Kingdom and the United States. The European Union takes part in the work of the OECD.

OECD Publishing disseminates widely the results of the Organisation's statistics gathering and research on economic, social and environmental issues, as well as the conventions, guidelines and standards agreed by its members.

OECD PUBLISHING, 2, rue André-Pascal, 75775 PARIS CEDEX 16
(22 2015 02 1 P) ISBN 978-92-64-24775-8 – 2016

www.ingramcontent.com/pod-product-compliance
Lightning Source LLC
LaVergne TN
LVHW081413110826

845149LV00010B/1729
9789264247758